Entertaining
Science Experiments
with Everyday Objects

Martin Gardner

Illustrated by
Anthony Ravielli

Dover Publications, Inc.
New York

Published in Canada by General Publishing Company, Ltd., 30 Lesmill Road, Don Mills, Toronto, Ontario.
Published in the United Kingdom by Constable and Company, Ltd., 10 Orange Street, London WC2H 7EG.

This Dover edition, first published in 1981, is a slightly corrected republication of the work first published by The Viking Press, N.Y., in 1960, under the title *Science Puzzlers*. The page of Selected References has been omitted in the present edition.

International Standard Book Number: 0-486-24201-3
Library of Congress Catalog Card Number: 81-67088

Manufactured in the United States of America
Dover Publications, Inc.
180 Varick Street
New York, N.Y. 10014

To
M. E. Hurst
a physics teacher
who taught
much more than physics

CONTENTS

INTRODUCTION

In selecting experiments for this volume, I have tried to keep in mind two guiding principles. First, avoid experiments requiring special equipment that cannot be found in an average home. Second, concentrate on experiments that, in addition to being amusing, astonishing, or entertaining, also teach something of importance about science.

Some of the stunts in this book, I must confess, were known to the ancient Greeks, but many are quite new and appear here for the first time inside a book. Who invents these clever diversions? I sometimes suspect that many of them are the brain-children of distinguished scientists who have not lost their boyhood spirit of play. Such a man was Robert W. Wood, a professor of physics at Johns Hopkins University. When he was not working on important projects or writing technical papers, Doctor Wood amused himself by playing practical jokes on his colleagues, exposing pseudo-scientists and spirit mediums, writing science fiction, and helping the police solve bombing mysteries. His quaint little book of drawings and verse, *How to Tell the Birds from the Flowers,* has been reprinted in paperback (New York: Dover Publications). Perhaps you have seen Paul Winchell, the television ventriloquist, ink a pair of eyes and a nose on his chin. The image of his face is inverted on the screen and Winchell wears on his head a dummy's costume that covers all of his face except the mouth and chin. The result is a weird, pinheaded creature with a flexible, gigantic mouth that grins when Winchell frowns and frowns when Winchell grins. This stunt was invented by none other than the fabulous Professor Wood.

Several decades ago, when there was a spirited public debate over whether pitched baseballs could really be made to curve, Wood devised a simple demonstration. He took a large, flat rubber band, cut it to make one long strip, then wound it tightly around a Ping-pong ball. By holding the free end of the band he was able to snap the ball forward, at the same time imparting to it a strong spin. The curving of the ball's path was clearly visible. (This stunt was not included in this collection because huge flat rubber bands are hard to come by, but Bernoulli's principle, which explains why baseballs curve, is easily demonstrated with a spool and card as explained on page 109).

To get the greatest value from this collection, try to follow up the experiments with exploratory reading. For example, after you have learned how to release a tangled couple (page 49), look up "topology" in a modern encyclopedia. Better still, read the chapter on it in the fascinating book, *Mathematics and the Imagination*, by James Newman and Edward Kasner (New York: Simon and Schuster, 1940). Don't just set fire to a lump of sugar (page 19) and then forget about it. See what you can learn about catalysts and the role they play in important chemical changes.

One other suggestion. If you want to entertain your friends—and some of the experiments in this book are superb party stunts—practice them a few times before you demonstrate. "Harpooning" a raw potato with a soda straw, for instance, is an amazing parlor trick, but you may have to damage many straws before you get the knack. Sherwood Anderson wrote a famous short story, "The Triumph of the Egg," about a restaurant owner who failed miserably in trying to show a customer how to put an egg into a bottle (see page 101). If the poor fellow had only practiced his trick a few times, he might not have forgotten what to do to make it work.

If you know, or should you invent, an unusual science experiment that is not in this collection, drop me a note about it in care of the publisher. I can't promise that I will find time to answer your letter, but I shall be most grateful, and perhaps I will be able to use your stunt in a second collection.

—MARTIN GARDNER

Entertaining
Science Experiments
with Everyday Objects

WATCH BECOMES COMPASS

Did you know that a watch can be used as a reliable compass on any day the sun is visible? Simply hold the watch flat and point the hour hand in the direction of the sun as shown. Imagine a line running from the center of the watch through a point midway between the hour hand and the number twelve. This line will point south.

The rule to remember is this: Before twelve noon, you bisect the angle formed by going counterclockwise from the number twelve to the hour hand. After twelve noon, you bisect the angle formed by going clockwise from the number twelve to the hour hand.

A little astronomical reflection should make clear why this works. In our hemisphere, the sun is due south at noon. If at that time we point the hour hand at the sun, both the hand and the number twelve will point south. Before that time, the sun will lie counterclockwise from the number twelve, and after that time, clockwise. During the twenty-four hours from twelve noon to twelve noon, the sun will make a complete circle back to its starting point, but the hour hand will make *two* circles in the same direction around the dial. Thus, the distance the hour hand travels, and the angle determined by its travel, must be halved.

On the other side of the equator the number twelve must be pointed at the sun. The angle between this number and the hour hand will then indicate *north*.

OATMEAL-BOX PLANETARIUM

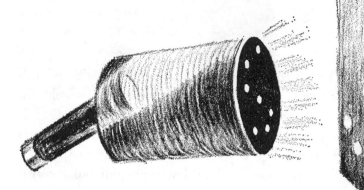

Cylindrical cardboard boxes, of the type at least one brand of oatmeal comes in, can be used for projecting beautiful images of star constellations on the wall or ceiling. Copy the constellation you wish to study on a sheet of thin paper. (You can find star charts in books on astronomy or accompanying an article on constellations in an encyclopedia.) Place the drawing face down on the outside of the bottom of the box. You should be able to see the star dots through the paper. With a nail, punch holes through the box at each dot. These holes form a mirror-image pattern of the constellation, but it will appear normal when projected.

To operate your "planetarium," take it into a dark room and insert a flashlight into the open end. Tilt the flashlight so it shines against the *side* of the box rather than directly toward the holes. This will throw an enlarged image of the constellation on the wall. By turning the box you can study all positions of the configuration.

How many times does the earth rotate during one complete journey around the sun? The answer depends on your point of view. As seen from the sun, the earth makes 365¼ turns. But as seen from a fixed star, it rotates 366¼ times. So the "sidereal day" (a rotation relative to a star) is a bit shorter than a "solar day."

The extra rotation is easily explained by the following simple experiment. Place two pennies flat on a table, edges touching, as shown. Hold the lower coin firmly with your left forefinger while you rotate the other penny around it (the edges should touch at all times). After the penny is back where it started, how many somersaults has Lincoln's head made? The surprising answer is not one but two. To an observer on the central penny, the outside penny would rotate only once, but to you, the "sidereal" observer, an additional rotation has occurred.

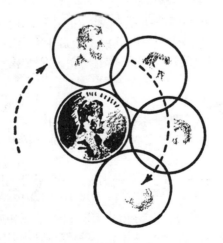

The word "catalyst" is used in chemistry for any substance that causes a chemical reaction to take place in its presence, but that doesn't itself take part in the reaction. This can be demonstrated easily with a sugar cube, a tiny amount of cigar or cigarette ash, and matches.

First put the sugar cube on a dish and see if you can set fire to it with a match. You'll find it impossible to do.

Now rub a bit of ash on one side of the cube and try again. This time it catches fire and burns steadily!

The ash, of course, is the catalyst. Its presence causes the sugar to ignite, although the ash itself is not combustible and remains unchanged throughout the burning.

LIFT THAT CUBE

A single ice cube is floating in a glass of water. You hold a piece of string about four inches long. Problem: without touching the ice with your fingers, lift the cube out of the glass with the string.

This puzzle should be presented at the dinner table where a salt shaker is available, for the solution makes use of the fact that salt causes ice to melt. Lay the string across the cube, as shown. Sprinkle salt on top of the ice. The ice around the string will start to melt. But in doing so, it will lose heat, and the cold ice cube will cause the salt water to freeze again. After a minute or two, lift the string. The cube will adhere tightly to it!

There is a lesson here for anyone who sprinkles salt on an icy sidewalk. Unless you use enough salt to melt *all* the ice, the water will freeze again.

With the aid of this fluid, newspaper photographs and cartoons can be transferred easily from the newsprint to blank sheets of paper. To make the fluid, mix four parts of water with one part of turpentine. Add a bit of soap about the size of a pencil eraser and shake the mixture until the soap is dissolved. The purpose of the soap is to form an emulsion that keeps the turpentine and water (which have different specific gravities) from separating.

To copy a newspaper picture, moisten the picture with the liquid, place a blank sheet of paper on top, then rub the paper vigorously with the bowl of a spoon. The turpentine dissolves enough of the ink so that a reverse impression of the picture is transferred to the paper.

21

PHYSIOLOGY

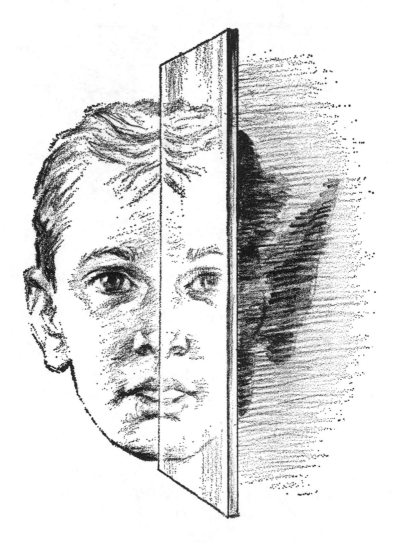

SPLIT PERSONALITY

Fifty years ago a German school of crank psychologists maintained that every individual has two basic sides to his personality and that the two sides could be revealed by this simple test. Obtain a front-view photograph of the person to be analyzed and a pocket mirror (preferably one without a frame). Place the edge of the mirror vertically on the center of the face, as shown. You will see a composite face formed from two left sides of the photograph. Turn the mirror the other way and you will see a composite face formed from two right sides of the picture.

These two "test faces" were supposed to indicate the two sides of the individual's personality. For example, one face may look happy and the other sad. Today no reputable psychologist takes this seriously. But the test is nevertheless interesting, because it proves that the two sides of most faces are not nearly so much alike as one would suppose. Try the test on your own picture. You'll be amazed at how different your "two" faces are.

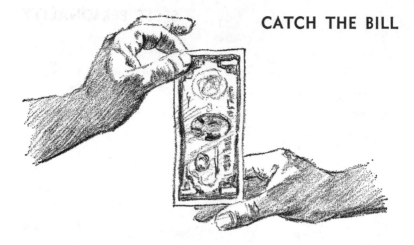

CATCH THE BILL

Hold a dollar bill in your left hand as shown, your right hand poised to catch the bill, but with fingers and thumb not quite touching it. If you release the bill, you'll find it easy to catch with your right hand before it falls to the floor.

Now, see if someone else can catch the bill when you release it. Let him place his thumb and fingers on either side of the bill, as you did before. Drop the bill. His fingers will close on empty air. You can repeat this as often as you wish. Chances are he won't be able to catch the bill.

The reason why the trick is so easy when you try it on yourself is that your brain is able to send "release" and "catch" signals simultaneously to your two hands. But when you hold the bill for someone else to catch, his brain must first see the bill fall, *then* send a catch signal to his fingers. This takes just a trifle too long to permit a successful catch.

PULSE DETECTOR

There are many kinds of expensive equipment, costing hundreds of dollars, for translating the human heartbeat into some sort of visual phenomenon. This simple device, costing less than a penny, will enable you to see your own heartbeat quite distinctly.

Just stick a thumbtack into the base of a large wooden kitchen match and balance it on your wrist, at the spot where you can feel the pulse. The arm should be resting comfortably on a table. The head of the match will vibrate slightly, like a tiny metronome, with each pulsation of your heart.

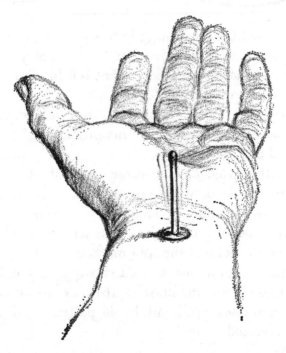

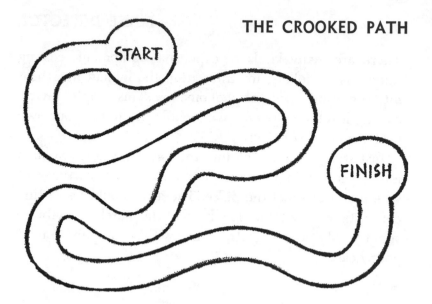

Drawing pictures or printing letters is enormously difficult for a young child. The reason: he has not yet built up a store of conditioned reflexes that tell him how to move his hand to produce a desired visual effect. Here's an amusing way to put yourself in the child's place and experience something akin to his problems of co-ordinating hand and eye.

Place this page on a dresser in front of the mirror. Pile some books between you and the page, so that you can see the page only by looking over the books and into the mirror. Reach around the books with a pencil in hand, and place the point at the spot marked "Start." Now see if, looking only *in the mirror*, you can trace the entire path without going over the borders. It isn't easy, because your deeply ingrained eye-hand habit patterns fail to apply to the reversed image.

ONE OR TWO POINTS?

Bend open a hairpin until its points are about an inch and a half apart. Ask someone to close his eyes and tell you whether you are pressing one or both points of the hairpin against his forearm. Surprisingly, he'll be unable to distinguish one sensation from the other. The widely separated points will feel exactly like a single point.

Now close the hairpin until its points are only $\frac{1}{16}$ of an inch apart. Repeat the same test on the subject's finger tips. This time, he'll have no difficulty distinguishing one from two points.

Different parts of the body vary enormously in their ability to distinguish separate points of pressure. You can, if you wish, make a chart of body sensitivity.

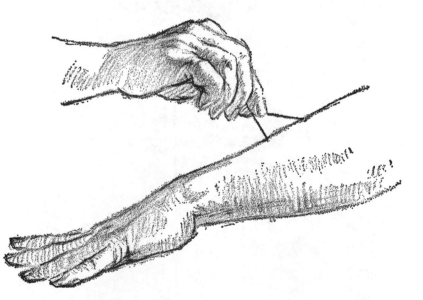

PSYCHOLOGY

To see this curious optical illusion, first place the tips of your index fingers together, holding them about three inches in front of your eyes as shown. Look *past* the fingers, focusing your eyes on something in the distance.

Now separate the tips of your fingers about half an inch. You'll see a "wienie"-shaped finger, with a nail at each end, floating, all by itself, in the air between your finger tips!

This is what happens. By focusing on a distant point, you prevent the separate images of your fingers (one image in each eye) from fusing properly. The position of your hands is such that your left eye's image of your left finger and your right eye's image of your right finger partially overlap to form the solid-looking "wienie" that seems to be floating in space.

CIRCLES ON THE CARD

Draw four heavy lines on a file card or rectangular piece of cardboard, as shown. Push a pin through the center and, holding the pin, spin the card. Surprisingly, you will see two concentric circles.

This puzzling illusion arises from the fact that there is a spot on each line which traces a smaller circle than any other spot while the card is spinning. This results in a maximum concentration of blackness along this circle, making it visible.

The trick works with only one set of lines, but drawing a second set opposite the first will strengthen the illusion.

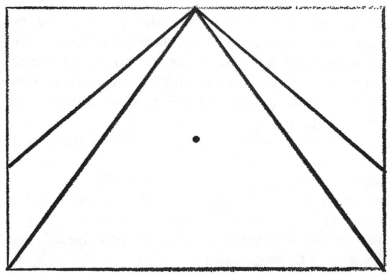

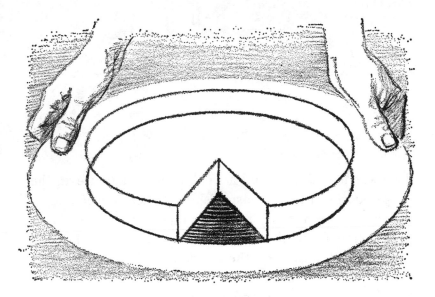

A slice is obviously missing from the cake in the next column. To find the piece, turn the picture upside down.

Here is the explanation of this startling optical illusion: When we turn the picture upside down, it is still possible to view it as an inverted cake with a missing slice. But since we almost never see a cake from this odd angle, our mind has an irresistible tendency to interpret the ellipses as the side of a cake pan viewed from above. As a result, the straight lines are seen as a solid slice of cake rather than as a depression left by a slice that has been removed.

31

THE PENETRATING MATCH

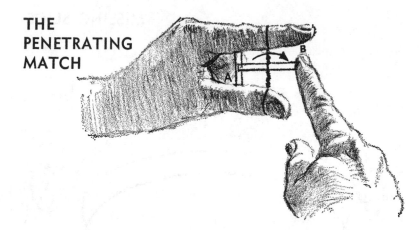

Two wooden matches and a small rubber band are all the props you need for this astonishing optical illusion.

Trim the head neatly from one match. Loop the elastic over your left thumb and forefinger, as shown. Put the headless match through the band, wind it very tightly in the direction of the arrow, and wedge a piece of the other match between thumb and finger to keep the first match from unwinding. Then, with the tip of your right forefinger, move match end A in the direction of the arrow. This will bring end B against the underside of the wedged match.

Now for the trick. Announce that when you say the magic word, end B will pass right through the wedged match. Say "Abracadabra" and raise your right forefinger just enough to allow B to snap back against your finger. Its motion will be so rapid that the movement will be invisible. With a little practice, you'll be able to keep the movement of your forefinger almost invisible, too, so that your audience will get the impression that one match has melted right through the other.

MOON ILLUSION

One of the most perplexing of all natural illusions is the apparent size of a full moon when seen low on the horizon. Six hours later, when almost overhead, its size seems to have diminished greatly. Yet, photographs show that the diameter of the disk is the same in both positions. The illusion persists even in a planetarium, with projected images of the moon.

Scientists do not agree on why this happens. The most widely accepted theory, which goes all the way back to the ancient Alexandrian astronomer Ptolemy, is that the horizon moon looks larger because we can contrast its size with such terrestrial objects as distant trees and houses. But this fails to explain why the illusion is just as strong at sea.

For a good discussion of the illusion see the cover article by Lloyd Kaufman and Irvin Rock in *Scientific American*, July 1962.

33

PENNY ILLUSION

Can you place a penny flat on this picture of a table in such a way that the penny does not touch any of the four sides of the table top?

It certainly looks possible, but when you try it, you will discover that the penny is too large. The illusion is caused partly by the angle of perspective in the drawing and partly by the fact that pennies are a trifle larger than we remember them to be.

SEE THROUGH YOUR HAND

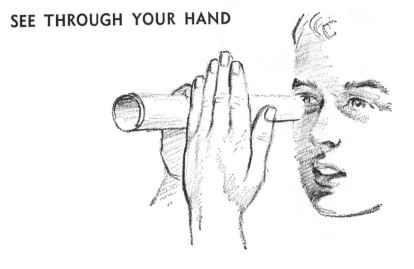

Roll a sheet of paper into a tube. Put one end of the tube to your right eye, like a telescope, and hold your left hand, palm toward you, against the tube. Both eyes must be kept open. Focus your vision on the opposite wall of the room. You will seem to be looking straight through a hole in your left hand! By sliding the hand back and forth along the tube, you can find a spot where it will look as though the hole is exactly in the center of the palm of your hand.

The illusion is the result of binocular vision. The out-of-focus image of the hand in your left eye overlaps what you see with your right eye.

If you shift your focus to your left hand, you will see the hole move away from the hand. Change the focus back to a distant object, and the hole moves back to the hand again.

GHOST PENNY

An interesting optical illusion is easily demonstrated with two pennies. Grip the pennies between the tips of your index fingers held vertically as shown in Fig. 1. Rub the pennies against each other with short, rapid, up and down movements. A *third* penny will mysteriously appear between and below the other two, as shown in Fig. 2.

The ghost penny is caused by a momentary retention on your retinas of images of the two coins in their lowest positions. But why the ghost penny always appears below and not above is a bit harder to understand.

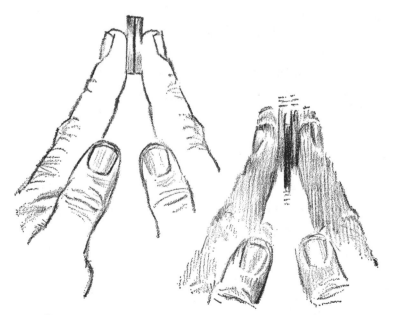

Would you doubt that the picture above shows a spiral line twisting out from the center? Trace any portion of it with the point of a pencil, and you'll discover that it is not a spiral. It is a series of concentric circles.

This remarkable optical illusion belongs to a class known as "twisted-cord illusions." They may be produced by twisting together a black and a white strand to make a single cord, then placing the twisted cord on variously patterned backgrounds. There are many theories, but there is no general agreement among psychologists as to why these illusions deceive the eye.

37

PAPER MOVIES

Cinematic motion is an illusion produced by a series of still images flashing rapidly across the screen. The principle is strikingly demonstrated with this paper toy.

Fold in half a paper rectangle, three by eight inches (Fig. 1). On the lower leaf draw the face shown in Fig. 2. On the upper leaf, draw the face in Fig. 3. Roll the upper leaf into a tube (Fig. 4).

Your left finger holds the upper left corner to a surface, while your right hand holds a pencil above the curled leaf, as shown. Move the pencil rapidly up and down, causing the curled leaf to unroll and roll up again. An amusing motion-picture effect will result.

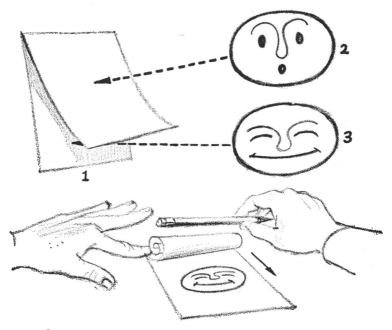

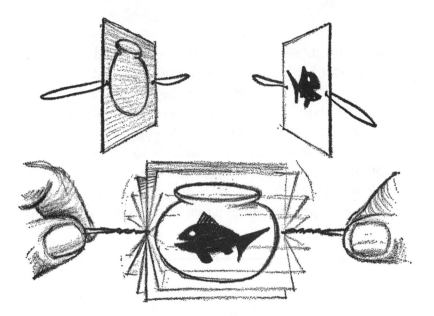

A thaumatrope is a toy device for demonstrating "retinal retention." This is the ability of the eye's retina to retain an image for a split second after the source of the image is withdrawn. A thaumatrope can be made as follows:

Cut out a square piece of cardboard, each edge of which measures about 1½ inches. Punch a hole near each of two opposite edges. Then attach short pieces of cord as shown. Draw a large fishbowl on one side of the square and a small fish on the other side. Hold a string between the thumb and first finger of each hand. By sliding the thumbs over the fingers, you can twirl the square rapidly. While it is twirling, you will see a composite picture of the fish inside the bowl.

PENCIL ILLUSIONS

An astonishing sensory illusion can be produced with a pencil. Hold it between your thumb and first finger, near one end as shown. Then move the hand straight up and down in short, quick shakes, covering a distance of no more than two inches. Don't try to wiggle the pencil with your thumb and finger. Just hold it in a loose grip so it wobbles slightly as your hand goes up and down. If this is done properly, the pencil will look exactly as though it were made of soft rubber that bends with every shake.

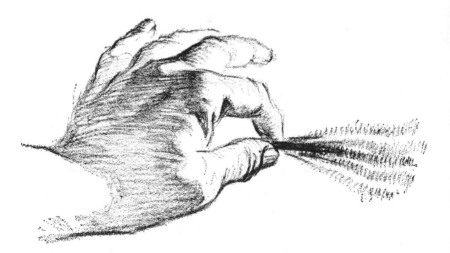

THE ILLUSORY PENDULUM

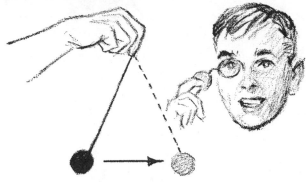

A startling, little-understood optical illusion can be demonstrated with a pendulum and a pair of dark glasses. Make the pendulum by tying a small object to one end of a two-foot length of string. Let someone stand across the room and swing the pendulum back and forth on a plane perpendicular to your line of vision.

View the pendulum by holding the spectacles so that only your right eye is seeing through a dark glass. *Both eyes must remain open.* The pendulum will appear to swing in a clockwise circle!

Now shift the dark glass to your left eye, keeping both eyes open as before. The pendulum will switch its direction of rotation and seem to swing counterclockwise!

The illusion arises from the fact that darkened retinal images are more slowly transmitted to the brain than bright images.

HOT OR COLD?

Before thermometers were invented, everyone judged how hot or cold something was by the way it felt. The following simple experiment shows how unreliable this method is.

Take three glasses. Fill one with very hot water, another with ice water, the third with water at room temperature. Put a finger of one hand in the hot water, a finger of the other hand in the cold. Hold them there for about a minute. Then use the two fingers, one at a time, to test the temperature of the glass of water at room temperature. This water will feel warm to the finger that has been in cold water, but quite cool to the finger that has been in hot water.

Judging subjectively (by personal reaction) rather than objectively (by scientific measurement) is one of the commonest causes of error. When you are in a hurry to get somewhere in a car, doesn't the traffic seem to move with annoying slowness? But when you're out for a Sunday drive, what a rush everyone else seems to be in!

43

If you glanced at the triangle above and read the words within it as "Paris in the spring," you'd better take a second look.

The fact is that most of us read by seeing certain word patterns as a whole (psychologists call this unified pattern a *Gestalt*), rather than by looking at each word individually. People who read rapidly in such fashion make poor proof-readers because their eyes slide rapidly over mistakes like the repeated word in the triangle.

You can have a lot of fun showing this triangle to your friends. You'll be surprised how many can't read it correctly even after a sixth or seventh look.

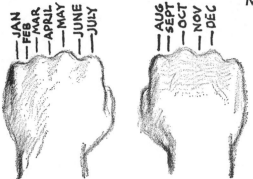

Hard-to-remember bits of information can often be stored in the memory by using mnemonic (memory) aids. Here are several examples of how it can be done:

Which side of a ship or airplane is the port side? You can remember that it is the left side, as you face forward, because "left" and "port" have the same number of letters. Is the port light red or green? Red, because port wine is red. Are stalactites or stalagmites found at the tops of caves? Stalac*tites* because they stick *tight* to cavern ceilings.

Mathematicians sometimes remember pi to seven decimal places by recalling the sentence, "May I have a large container of coffee?" The number of letters in each word stands for a corresponding digit of pi.

The illustration above shows how your fists may be used for remembering the number of days in each month. Mentally label the knuckles and the spaces between them, from left to right, with the names of the months in proper order. All knuckle months have 31 days. The others have 30, except February. It has 28 days, except in leap years, when it has 29.

45

GENERAL MATHEMATICS

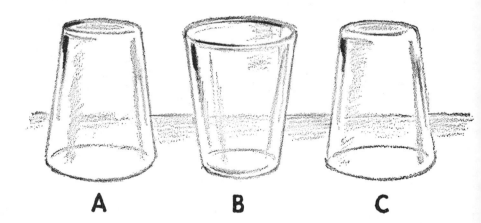

A   B   C

TOPSY-TURVY TUMBLERS

Here's an amusing mathematical trick to spring on your friends. Set three empty drinking glasses in a row on the table, center glass right side up and end glasses inverted, as shown. The idea is to turn two glasses at a time and, in exactly three moves, to get all of them right side up.

To demonstrate the procedure, seize glasses A and B, one in each hand, and turn them both over simultaneously. Do the same with glasses A and C, then repeat with A and B. Result: all three glasses are upright.

Now comes the sneaky part. Casually turn the center glass upside down, and challenge someone to get all three of the glasses right side up, as you have just done.

Chances are, no one will notice that the glasses are arranged differently than when *you* began. You started with two down, one up; now two are up, one down. The mathematics of the trick are such that, from this new starting formation, the puzzle can't be solved in *any* number of moves.

Your victims will be frustrated until some sharp-eyed spectator notices the skulduggery.

REVERSE TICKTACKTOE

A mathematical game can sometimes be reversed so that the object of play is to force the other player to win. This usually results in a surprisingly different mathematical structure. Giveaway checkers is a familiar example. Less well known is the reverse form of ticktacktoe. In this, the first player to get three marks in a row *loses*.

Reverse ticktacktoe is more complicated than the regular game. The second player has a strong advantage and can always win (if he plays correctly), unless the first player opens in the center cell. In that case, if the first player always takes a cell directly opposite his opponent's last move (so that three marks are in a line) the game is sure to end in a draw, as in the one shown.

The best plan to follow in playing against someone who does not know the symmetry strategy just explained is to play each time so that you leave your opponent a maximum number of ways to win. Try a few games, and see how much fun it is.

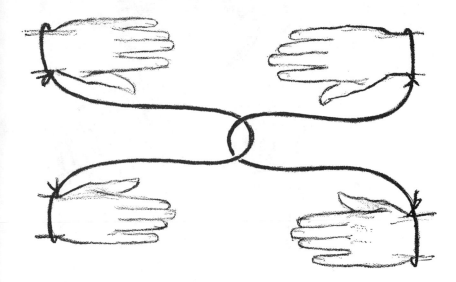

The study of knots and linkages belongs to a branch of geometry called topology. Here's a topological puzzle that makes an entertaining party game.

Divide the guests into couples. Each couple ties a piece of string to their wrists, with the two strings linked together as shown. A prize goes to the first couple to unlink themselves without cutting or untying the cord.

The puzzle is solved by passing the center of one string under the string around the other person's wrist, then over his hand, then back under the string again.

KNOTTY PROBLEM

Lay a piece of rope or cord out straight on a table. Challenge anyone to seize one end in each hand and tie a knot without letting go of either end.

It seems physically impossible, yet it can be done easily. The trick is to fold your arms first and then bend over and pick up the rope as shown. When you unfold your arms, an overhand knot will form in the center of the rope. It is interesting to note that two geometrically distinct types of knots can be tied in this manner, depending on whether you cross your right arm over the left or left over the right. The resulting knots are mirror images of each other.

50

Let's suppose that you marry and have four children. How many will be boys, and how many will be girls?

There are three possibilities: they may all be of one sex, there may be three of one sex and one of the other, or the sexes may be balanced two and two. Which possibility would you say was most likely?

Most people think the 2–2 combination is most likely, but the most probable combination is actually 3–1. You can prove this by making a list of the 16 possible permutations of four children, each of which may be male or female.

You will discover that eight of these are 3–1, giving a probability of 8:16, or 1:2 that the children would comprise three boys and one girl or three girls and one boy. Only six of the permutations are 2:2, making the probability of this event 6:16 or 3:8. The remaining possibility—that they would all be of one sex—occurs only twice on the list, giving it a probability of 2:16, or 1:8.

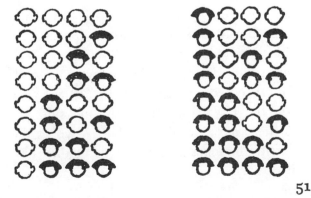

THE THREE CARDS

The odds of winning in certain games are often quite different from what you would expect. Suppose you have three cards: one is black on both sides (BB), one is white on both sides (WW), and one is black on one side and white on the other (BW). You shake them in a hat, then take out a card and place it on the table. What are the odds that the underside will match the upper?

If the top of the card is black, you might reason as follows: "This can't be the WW card. Since it is just as likely to be the BB as the BW, the odds that the underside is black must be even."

As a matter of fact, the odds are two to one! There are *three*, not two equally possible cases: (1) the visible black side is on the BW card; (2) it is one side of the BB; (3) it is the *other* side of the BB. In two of these cases the underside matches the upper, as against only one in which it doesn't.

Trisecting an angle, using only compass and straight edge, was one of the great classical problems of antiquity. Modern mathematics has proved it impossible, but here is a simple and ingenious mathematical device that trisects accurately.

Cut a piece of cardboard to the pattern shown in Fig. 1. Place the device on the angle so point A lies on one side of the angle, edge B intersects the angle's vertex, and the curved edge is tangent to the other side (Fig. 2). Make dots on the paper at points C and D, draw lines from the angle's vertex through the dots, and there you have it! If the angle is too acute for the device to fit, you can always double the angle, trisect it, then bisect each trisection to obtain trisections for the original angle.

Now see if you know your plane geometry well enough to *prove* that the instrument will trisect.

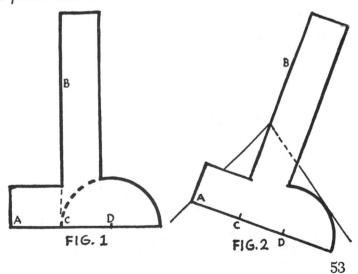

FIG. 1   FIG. 2 D

SPIN A HYPOCYCLOID

A hypocycloid is a curve traced by a point on the rim of a circle when that circle is rolled around the inside rim of a larger circle. For example, Fig. 1 shows a three-cusped hypocycloid, called the "deltoid," that results when the rolling circle has a diameter one-third that of the larger circle.

See if you can guess the shape of a hypocycloid generated by a small circle with a diameter exactly one-half that of the large circle (Fig. 2). Then test your intuition by cutting a cardboard circle of the right size and rolling it around the inside of the rim of a circular pie pan. You'll be surprised at the answer!

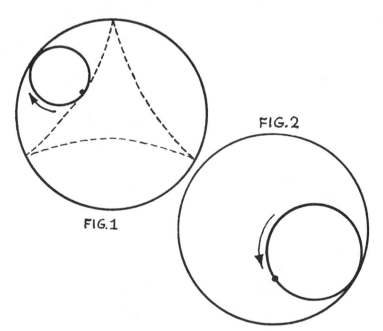

FIG. 2

FIG. 1

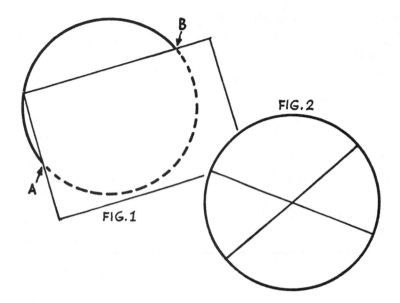

FIG.2

FIG.1

In most geometry classes, you are taught to find the center of a given circle by a fairly complicated compass procedure. Here's a short-cut method used by commercial artists. It often comes in handy.

Place the corner of a sheet of paper on the circle's circumference (Fig. 1), then mark points A and B where the sides of the paper intersect the circle. The position of the sheet does not matter in the least. Points A and B are certain to mark the ends of a diameter.

Use the edge of the paper to rule in lightly the diameter, then repeat the procedure at a different spot to get another diameter (Fig. 2). The two lines intersect at the circle's center.

DRAW A PERFECT ELLIPSE

A circle is easily drawn with a compass, but how would you go about drawing a perfect ellipse? Here's an easy method.

Stick two pins in a sheet of paper. Tie a string into a loop and put the loop over the pins. Stretch the string taut with the point of your pencil, as shown. Then move the pencil around the pins. It will trace a perfect ellipse.

This technique demonstrates the fundamental geometrical property of the ellipse: lines drawn from the two foci to any point on the ellipse always have a constant sum. In this case, the pins are at the foci, and string segments AC and BC are the two lines to a common point on the curve. Since segment AB stays the same length, the sum of AC and BC must remain constant while your pencil traces the curve.

As you move the pins closer together, keeping the same size loop, you'll find that the pencil traces broader and broader ellipses. When the foci come together, you'll have a circle.

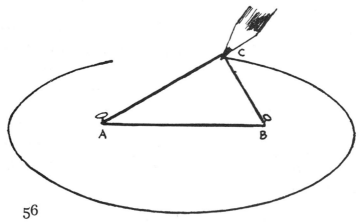

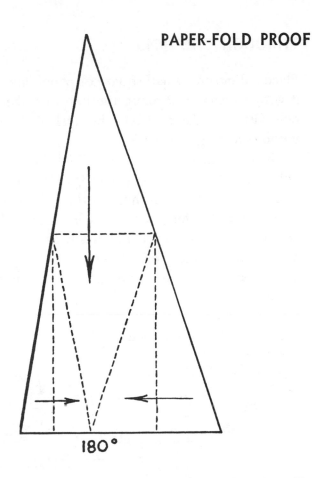

180°

Your geometry teacher may not approve of this absurdly simple way to prove that the sum of all the angles of a triangle is equal to a straight (180-degree) angle. All the same, the proof is quite convincing.

Cut a triangle of any size or shape out of a piece of paper. By folding over the corners, as shown, you can easily make the three angles fit neatly together to form a straight angle at the triangle's base.

THROUGH THE HOLE

Place a dime on a small square of paper, and trace around it with a pencil. Cut along the line to make a dime-sized hole (Fig. 1). Can a quarter be pushed through this hole without tearing the paper?

The surprising answer is yes. Fold the paper across the hole, with the quarter inside (Fig. 2). It is now a simple matter to push the coin through the hole, as shown in Fig. 3. In similar fashion you can push a half dollar through a hole the size of a nickel. For the trick to work, it is only necessary that the circumference of the hole be a trifle more than twice the diameter of the coin to be passed through it.

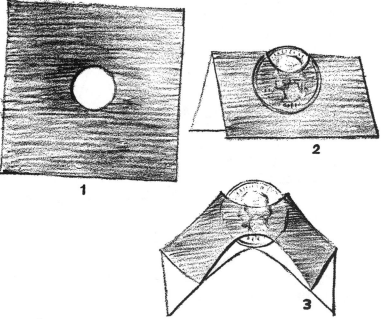

58

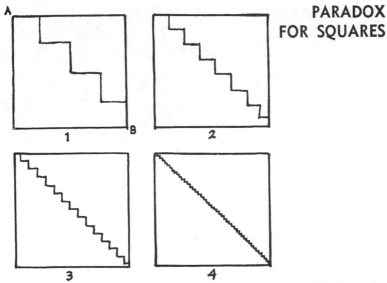

The four figures illustrate an amusing "proof" that the diagonal of a square is equal in length to twice the square's side!

Suppose the square to be 100 units on the side. In Fig. 1, we drew a zigzag path from corner A to corner B, making each step 25 units broad and 25 units high. The length of this path is clearly 200 units, which is twice the square's side. In Fig. 2, the steps are shortened to 20 units, but the length of the path remains the same. In fact, it remains 200 units no matter how small we make the steps (Figs. 3 and 4), provided the sides of each step are parallel to the sides of the square. Eventually the steps become so minute that the path apparently will become a straight line. But it will still be 200 units long!

The explanation is that no matter how small the steps are made, they will never vanish. In other words, the zigzag path will never become a straight line.

59

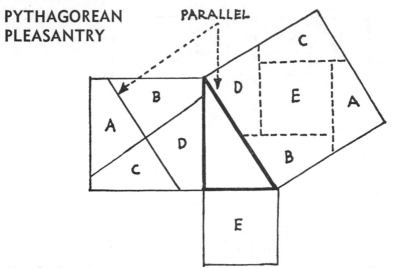

Hundreds of ingenious proofs have been devised for the famous Pythagorean theorem, or forty-seventh proposition of Euclid, which states that the square on the hypotenuse of a right-angled triangle equals the sum of the squares on the other two sides. Here is a highly unorthodox but convincing way to demonstrate the theorem with the aid of a pair of scissors.

First draw the squares on the two shorter sides of any right-angled triangle. Divide the square on the larger of these sides into four parts by two lines at right angles to each other and intersecting at the center of the square. One of these lines must be parallel to the triangle's hypotenuse.

Now cut out the small square and the four parts of the larger one. You'll find that these five pieces will fit together neatly to form the square on the hypotenuse! Now that you have *demonstrated* the theorem, can you *prove* it mathematically?

If you add all the digits of a number and subtract the total from the original number, you'll find that the answer will always be a multiple of nine. An entertaining mind-reading trick can be based on this curious fact.

Hand an unused folder of paper matches to someone. Turn your back and request him to follow these instructions:

1. Tear out any number of matches from 1 to 10 and put them *in his pocket.*

2. Count the remaining matches, add the two digits of this number, and tear out matches that correspond to this total. For example: if he counts 16 matches in the folder, 1 plus 6 is 7, so he tears out 7 matches. These matches are also *pocketed.*

3. Tear out any number of the remaining matches, this time holding them *in his fist.*

You turn around, glance at the open folder, and tell him the number of matches he is holding *in his fist.*

The secret: step 2 above will always leave 9 matches. Count the matches left in the folder and subtract from 9 to learn the number he has concealed in his fist.

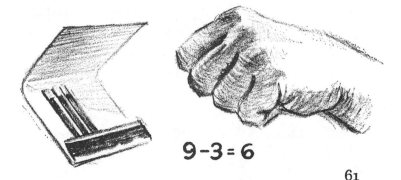

9-3=6

8+7=15

The fact that opposite sides of a die always total seven underlies many unusual mathematical tricks with dice. Here is one of the best:

Turn your back while someone tosses three dice. Ask him to: (1) add all the uppermost faces; (2) pick up one die and add the *bottom* face to the former total; (3) roll this same die again and add the number it shows on top to the previous total.

Turn around and point out that you have absolutely no way of knowing which of the three dice was used for the second roll. Pick up the dice, shake them in your hand a moment, and then announce the correct total!

How do you know? Simple. Merely total the top faces of the three dice before you pick them up, and add seven. With a little thinking, you should be able to see why this works.

Ask someone to jot down any three-digit number in which the first and last digits differ by at least 2. Suppose he writes 317. Tell him to reverse the digits and subtract the smaller number from the larger (713 minus 317 leaves 396). Finally, he must reverse the digits in this answer and add them to the answer (693 plus 396 equals 1089).

"Now, if you will please breathe on that windowpane," you say to him, pointing to one of the windows in the room, "you'll see your final answer on the glass." When he breathes on the glass, the number 1089 magically appears on the misted pane!

The secret is quite simple: the answer is always 1089.

Before doing the trick, mix some detergent in a glass of water, dip your finger in the liquid, and write 1089 with the tip of your finger on the windowpane. The writing is invisible when dry, but when someone breathes on the glass the area touched by your finger will not fog.

LIGHTNING ADDITION

Anyone can be a lightning-fast calculator if he knows the secret of this addition trick:

Ask someone to write any five-figure number on the blackboard. You then write a five-figure number beneath it, apparently at random. Actually, you choose your digits so that each one, added to the digit above it, will total nine. For example:

His number: 45623
Your number: 54376

Tell the person to put a third five-figure number beneath your number. You then write a fourth number, using the same nine-principle. After he has written a fifth number, you draw a line under it and without a moment's hesitation write the correct total. More startling still, you write it from left to right!

How do you do it? Just subtract 2 from the fifth number and put 2 in front of what is left. For example: if the fifth number is 48765, the total will be 248763.

In parts of Russia, peasants still use their fingers as "digital computers" (an appropriate name!) for multiplying numbers from 6 through 10. The method is interesting. Want to try it?

Mentally number your fingers from 6 to 10, as shown in Fig. 1. Suppose you wish to multiply 7 by 8. The tip of a 7-finger (on either hand) is placed against the tip of the 8-finger on the other hand (Fig. 2). The touching fingers, together with all fingers below them on both hands, represent tens. In this case there are 5 such fingers. Five tens are 50.

The next step is to multiply the number of remaining fingers on the left hand by the number of remaining fingers on the right. Three times 2 is 6. Then add 6 to 50 to obtain the final answer: 56. The method never fails.

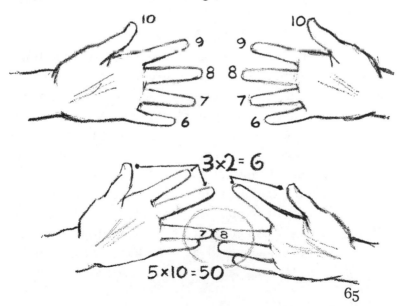

CRAZY MULTIPLICATION

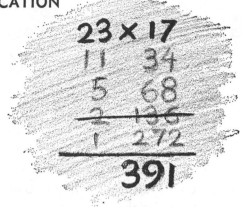

$$23 \times 17$$

11	34
5	68
~~2~~	~~136~~
1	272

391

There are many methods of multiplying numbers of more than one digit. Here is one of the strangest.

Suppose you wish to multiply 23 by 17. Half of 23 is 11½. Ignore the fraction, and put 11 under 23 as shown. Half of 11 is 5½. Again ignore the fraction, and put down 5. In short, form a column of successive divisions by 2, omitting all remainders. Continue until you reach 1.

Form a corresponding column under 17. But this time double each number to obtain the one below. Continue until you have a number opposite the 1 in the left-hand column. Draw a line through any row (in this case there is only one) that has an even number on the left. Now add the numbers remaining in the right-hand column. Believe it or not, the answer will be the product of 23 and 17. The method is based on the binary number system and works with any pair of numbers, no matter how large.

Why it works is too complicated to detail here. But if you are interested, you will find it clearly explained in Chapter 3 of Helen Merrill's *Mathematical Excursions.*

66

MAGIC MULTIPLICATION

Here's an amusing number trick to show your friends.

First jot down on a sheet of paper the "magic number" 12,345,679. It's an easy number to remember because it consists simply of all the digits (numbers from 1 through 9) in serial order with the 8 omitted.

Now ask a friend to tell you his favorite digit. Whatever number he chooses, multiply it in your head by 9 and write the result beneath the magic number. For example, if he tells you his favorite digit is 3, you put 27 below the magic number. Then ask him to multiply 12,345,679 by 27. The answer is sure to astound him, for it will consist entirely of 3's—the very digit he selected!

The trick works just as well with any digit. Try it and see.

A popular novelty in Japan is a glass with a picture on the bottom that is invisible until the glass is filled. Such a glass can be made easily with dime-store materials. You will need a thick-sided glass jigger (the interior of which narrows to about the size of the tip of your finger), a *transparent* glass marble about ½ inch to ¾ inch in diameter, and some quick-drying cement. Transparent glass marbles are sold in various colors for use in goldfish bowls.

Drop the marble into the jigger, then with a toothpick put a ring of cement around the marble, where it touches the glass, to hold it firmly in place. Paste a small picture on the outside bottom of the glass, picture side toward the glass. If you wish, paint the outside bottom of the glass black to conceal the fact that something is pasted there.

When you look down into the glass you will see nothing, because the picture is beyond the focal length of the marble. But when you fill the glass with water, the picture appears suddenly in magnified form! The reason for this is that liquids have a much higher refractive index than air. This alters the focal length of the sphere, or marble, causing it to act as a convex lens focused on the picture.

UNREVERSED IMAGE

When you look into a mirror, you don't see yourself the way others see you. You see a reversed image. If you part your hair on the left, your image parts its hair on *its* right, and so on.

With the aid of two pocket mirrors (preferably without frames), you can actually see your face the way others see it. Hold the mirrors at right angles to each other and look directly into them as shown. You'll be able to adjust the mirrors until they form a perfect reflection of your face.

Now, wink your right eye. Your image will wink its right eye, just the opposite of what you would see in an ordinary mirror. The reason is that each mirror reflects the image in the other, so that what you see is actually a reflection of a reflection, or a reversal of a reversal, which of course is the same as no reversal at all.

COLOR THAT ISN'T THERE

"Subjective color" is the term physicists apply to colors that appear when you are watching rapidly alternating patterns of black and white. To demonstrate this puzzling phenomenon, copy the circle shown and mount it on cardboard. Push a pin through the center dot so you can spin the disk.

While the disk is whirling you will see concentric circles richly tinted with different colors! Reverse the direction of spin and the order of colors will also reverse!

Gustav Fechner, a nineteenth-century German physicist, was the first to construct such a disk. Since then, physicists have been unable to agree on just what causes these curious color sensations. A few years ago, a Chicago television performer spun a large wheel of this type, and people watching his program saw the colors quite clearly on their black-and-white television screens.

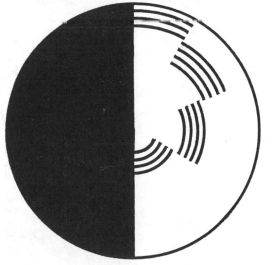

SWIZZLE-STICK CODE

To decode the secret message below, you must use a solid, cylindrical, transparent glass or plastic rod. Dime stores sell them to be used for stirring mixed drinks. Hold the rod over the printing, close to the page, and the message will be readable through the rod.

The code used in the message is based on the fact that when you look at printing through the rod, its refractive power reverses each letter and at the same time inverts it. So all you have to do is print your message in the following code:

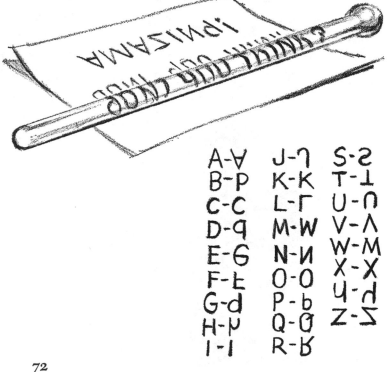

A-Ɐ	J-ꝛ	S-ꙅ
B-ꓭ	K-K	T-⊥
C-Ɔ	L-Γ	U-∩
D-ꓷ	M-W	V-∧
E-Ǝ	N-И	W-M
F-Ⅎ	O-O	X-X
G-ꓷ	P-b	Ƴ-�
H-ꓭ	Q-Ꝺ	Z-Ƨ
I-I	R-Я	

MAKE A STROBOSCOPE

A stroboscope is a device that cuts off light at regular intervals of time. When you look through it at a rhythmically moving object, the motion seems to slow down or even to stop. A simple stroboscope is easily made by cutting eight narrow slots at evenly spaced intervals around the rim of a cardboard circle. Put a pin through the center, and stick the pin into the eraser of a pencil so you can spin the disk in front of one eye, as shown.

Look through the moving rim at a rotating object—a spinning phonograph record, electric fan, or even a mirror reflection of the stroboscope itself. Depending on the relative speeds of the stroboscope and object, the object will appear to be stationary or to move slowly in the direction of its actual spin or to move slowly in the opposite direction. This is because you see the object only at regularly spaced instants and do not see its movements in between.

Stroboscopic illusions are frequent in motion pictures, because the movie camera takes its series of pictures at evenly spaced intervals.

73

WATERMARK WRITING

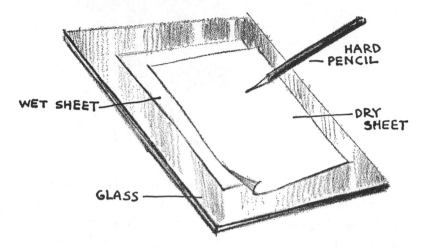

As every stamp collector knows, a watermark is an invisible imprint on a postage stamp, for identification purposes. It becomes visible when the stamp is immersed in liquid. Watermarks are produced by applying pressure that mashes the fibers of the paper and thus changes the way they reflect light when wet. Watermarks are easy to make and provide a novel, little-known way to write secret messages.

Dip a sheet of blank paper in water, place it on a smooth, hard surface (such as a windowpane or mirror), and cover it with a dry sheet. Write on the dry sheet, using a hard lead pencil and firm pressure. Discard the dry sheet. You will find the writing clearly visible on the wet one. The writing will vanish without a trace when the paper dries, but will reappear when the sheet is dipped in water.

VANISHING POSTAGE STAMP

Place a postage stamp face up on a table. Set a glass of water on the stamp. Then cover the glass with a saucer, as shown. The stamp disappears! Walk around the glass, peering into it from any angle you please. The stamp is completely invisible.

The explanation lies in the phenomenon of refraction— the bending of light rays when they pass at an angle from one medium to another. The dotted lines show how light rays are refracted upward when they pass from water to air and how they strike the underside of the saucer. Since the saucer screens off all refracted rays, there is no angle from which the postage stamp can be seen.

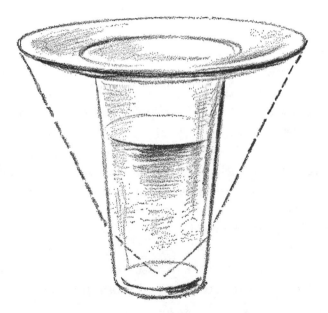

SPECTRUM ON THE CEILING

One of Isaac Newton's most famous experiments was done with a beam of sunlight passing through a prism to form rainbow colors on the wall. You can perform a similar experiment with a flashlight, a pocket mirror, and a shallow bowl of water.

Place the mirror in the bowl so it is at an angle of about 30 degrees to the surface of the water. Darken the room, and then shine a flashlight toward the mirror. A small spectrum of colors will appear on the ceiling.

The experiment proves that white light is composed of many different wave lengths, each belonging to a different color. The water acts as a prism, refracting each wave length at a slightly different angle to form the colors on the ceiling.

FAR OR NEAR?

The only clue at the scene of the crime was a pair of spectacles. Sherlock Dolmes held them a foot or two from his eyes. "Hmmm," he said. "The murderer was farsighted in his left eye, nearsighted in his right, with a bit of astigmatism in both."

"Great Scott!" cried Matson. "How did you deduce that?"

"Elementary, my dear Matson. When a lens magnifies objects seen through it, it is a convex lens intended to correct farsightedness. When the lens diminishes objects, it is concave and intended to correct nearsightedness. And if objects change shape when you rotate the lens slowly around its center, you know the lens is for astigmatism."

These tests are worth knowing. When an eye doctor writes a prescription for glasses he uses a plus sign to indicate a convex lens, a minus sign for a concave one. Sometimes a careless optician misreads the signs. With these simple tests a person who wears glasses can make sure that no error of this type has been committed.

PICTURE COPIER

We are familiar with the fact that a pane of window glass will reflect images like a mirror, especially at night when the far side of the window is dark and the room is illuminated. This fact can be put to practical use in making an excellent device for copying drawings.

Simply arrange for a plate of glass (the glass in an empty picture frame will do) to be supported vertically on a table, as shown. Put the picture to be copied on one side of the glass, a sheet of blank paper on the other. Sit on the side where the picture is. Darken the room except for one lamp that shines on the picture. The image of the picture will seem to fall on the blank paper. The glass will be transparent enough for you to see your hand and pencil through it while you trace the image.

An interesting physiological experiment, known as "Meyer's experiment," can be performed easily with a sheet of colored paper, a small square of gray cardboard, and a sheet of wax paper from a kitchen roll.

Place the cardboard square on the colored paper (a bright red or green works best). Then cover both paper and square with wax paper folded once, twice, or three times, depending on its thickness. The square, seen through the transparent paper, will appear strongly tinted with a color complementary to the color of the paper. That is, it will seem light green if red paper is used, pinkish if green paper is used.

The effect is closely related to the fact, familiar to all artists, that shadows of colored objects acquire a tint of the complementary color. A classic discussion of Meyer's experiment will be found in Chapter 17 of William James's *Principles of Psychology* (available as a paperback published by Dover Publications).

COLORED PAPER

GRAY CARDBOARD

FOLDED WAX PAPER

GRAVITY

If you overlap the prongs of two table forks, then insert a half dollar between the prongs so that it holds both forks, you'll be able to balance the coin and forks on the brim of a glass as shown.

This is extremely baffling to most people because the entire weight of both forks is on the outer portion of the coin. Why don't the forks and coin fall?

The explanation: The heavy handles of the forks curve *toward* the glass. This shifts the center of gravity of the entire structure to a point directly beneath the spot where the coin rests on the glass, putting the forks and coin in a state of stable equilibrium.

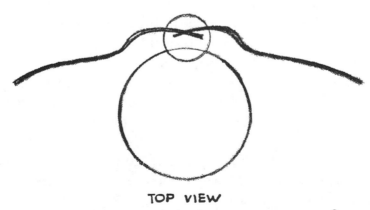

TOP VIEW

GRAVITY MACHINE

A perpetual-motion machine operated solely by gravity is impossible, but gravity does play an essential role in thousands of simple mechanical devices. Here is a gravity machine you can construct from a candle, a needle, two glasses, and two saucers.

Cut away the tallow at the bottom of a long candle to expose the wick. Push the needle through the middle of the candle; then rest the ends of the needle on the rims of two glasses. Place a saucer beneath each wick; then light the wicks.

As the tallow drips from the ends, one side soon becomes lighter than the other. Gravity then pulls down the heavy end, causing it to drip a larger amount of tallow on the saucer. This, of course, lightens that end, so it goes up while the other end goes down, deposits a blob of wax, and goes back up again. The candle will seesaw up and down for hours.

Does a bowl of water weigh more with a goldfish in it than it does without the fish? This question usually provokes considerable argument. The answer is yes. The bowl's weight is increased by exactly the weight of the fish inside it.

Suppose you merely poke a finger into the water. Most people would guess that this would not make the bowl heavier, but it does. The bowl's weight is increased by the weight of the water your finger displaces, as you can easily demonstrate.

Place a glass on each end of a ruler, with a pencil beneath, to form a crude balance scale, as shown. Adjust the pencil until the scale is almost, but not quite, balanced. Now plunge your finger into the raised glass, taking care to touch only the water. The extra weight will immediately tip the "scale" the other way.

GALILEO VS. ARISTOTLE

Everyone knows about Galileo's famous experiment of dropping unequal weights from the leaning tower of Pisa. The experiment proved that Aristotle was mistaken in his belief that heavy objects fall faster than lighter ones.

You can repeat this historic experiment on a small scale by dropping a half dollar and a tiny piece of paper. To eliminate air resistance on the paper, put it on top of the coin as shown. Drop the coin to the floor, giving it a slight spin to keep it horizontal while it falls. The coin and paper will fall together.

But, you may object, perhaps currents of air flowing around the falling coin cause the paper to stick to it. To prove this isn't so, hold the coin and paper high in the air. Then, instead of dropping the coin, carry it down at a speed faster than normal falling speed. The piece of paper will be left behind.

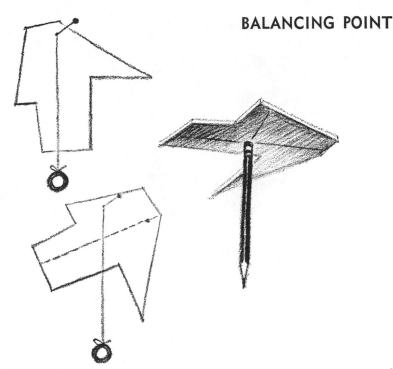

The center of gravity of an irregularly shaped piece of cardboard is the spot where it will balance on the eraser of a pencil. Here is an interesting way to locate this spot.

Punch a hole near the edge of the cardboard, and hang it on a nail. Make a plumb line by tying a weight to a piece of thread. Hang the thread on the nail, as shown, and mark the vertical line with a pencil. The center of gravity always seeks the lowest position it can reach, so you know it is somewhere on this vertical line.

Punch another hole at some other spot near the cardboard's edge and repeat the same procedure. The spot where the two lines cross must, of course, be the center of gravity.

85

THE FLOATING BALLOON

A gas-filled toy balloon of the type sold at fairs and on street corners can be made to hang suspended in the middle of a room, with no visible means of support. Here's how:

Tie a small piece of cardboard to the end of the balloon's string, as shown. Use a piece just heavy enough to keep the balloon from rising. With a pair of scissors, start snipping off tiny pieces of cardboard. In this way you can adjust the balloon's weight until it hangs magically in mid-air.

The trick would not work if it were not for the fact that cool air is heavier and denser than warm air and therefore has greater buoyancy. The balloon hangs at a point where it is too light to sink into the denser air, which stays in the lower part of the room, too heavy to rise into the warmer air above.

86

This curious little toy seems to defy gravity. When it is placed at the bottom of a sloping track, it actually runs uphill!

The toy is a double cone, easily made from two plastic funnels that can be bought at a five-and-ten-cent store. Use rubber cement to stick their rims together. The sloping track is cut from cardboard. You'll have to experiment to get the slope just right, since it will depend on the size of the funnels.

Arrange the track so the two sides are about an inch apart at the lower end, with a width at the other end equal to the length of the double cone. When the cone is placed at the bottom of this track, it slowly rolls to the top.

Observe the cone carefully from the side and you'll see what really happens. As the cone moves "up," the increasing width of the track lowers the cone so that its center of gravity actually moves down.

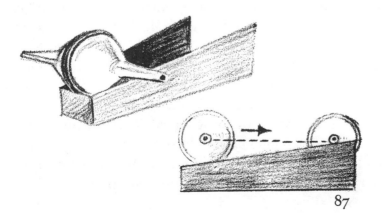

STATIC ELECTRICITY

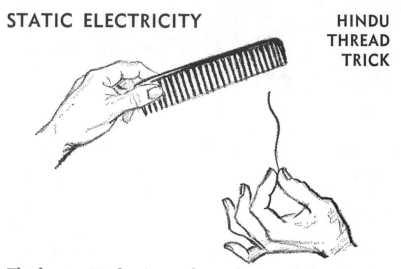

The famous Hindu rope trick may be a myth, but here's a miniature version of it that anyone can do. Hold one end of a short piece of thread. With your other hand, rub a pocket comb briskly on your clothing, then bring it near the free end of the thread. You'll find you can make the thread stand upright as shown. If you move the comb in small circles, the thread will also move in small circles.

Static electricity makes the trick possible. Friction causes free electrons to leave your clothing and attach themselves to the comb, giving it a negative electric charge. The thread behaves exactly like an electroscope. Free electrons are repelled from the thread, leaving it positively charged. Since opposite charges attract, it is drawn towards the negatively charged comb.

The trick works best on cold dry days. Water is such an excellent conductor of electricity that, if the air is too humid, there will be a rapid leakage of the electrical charge and the thread will not respond properly.

88

This is an amusing dinner-table stunt to show friends on dry winter days when static electricity is easy to produce. Shake a pile of salt on the tablecloth, flatten it with your finger, then shake some pepper on top of it. The problem is to remove the pepper from the salt.

Not many people are likely to think of the easy solution. Just put a static charge on a pocket comb by running it a few times through your hair. Bring one end of the comb to about an inch above the salt. The grains of pepper, which are lighter than salt grains, will jump to the comb.

89

THE INVISIBLE LEG

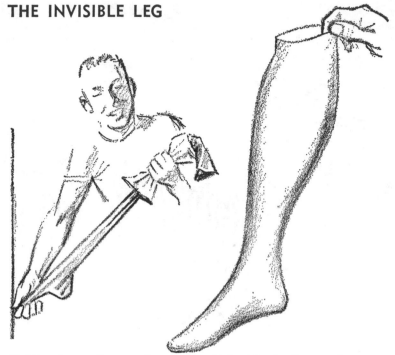

Cold winter days, when the air inside is dry and warm, are ideal for experiments with static electricity. Here is an unusual one.

Press the toe of a nylon stocking against the wall. With the other hand, stroke the stocking vigorously several times with a transparent polyethylene vegetable bag. (If you can stretch the material of the bag you know it's polyethylene.)

Now hold the stocking in the air and see how it fills out as though an invisible leg were inside. The effect is due to a strong static charge on the nylon. Because like charges repel each other, the sides of the stocking billow as far apart as possible.

You hear a lot these days about how electronic devices regulate themselves by "feedback." The principle of feedback isn't hard to understand. A wall thermostat, for example, "feeds back" to the furnace information about the temperature in a room, and the amount of heat is adjusted constantly to maintain a steady temperature.

For a demonstration of a simple feedback mechanism, try this stunt:

Rest the ends of a yardstick on your two index fingers as shown. Now bring the fingers slowly together, trying your best to make them meet at some spot *other* than the center of the stick. You will find it impossible.

Why? If one finger gets a trifle ahead of the other, the weight of the stick on that finger increases. This, in turn, increases the amount of friction between finger and stick, causing the stick to stop sliding until the other finger catches up. In short, the stick serves as a feedback device. By slowing up a finger that starts to get ahead, it keeps the fingers moving toward its center at approximately equal rates of speed.

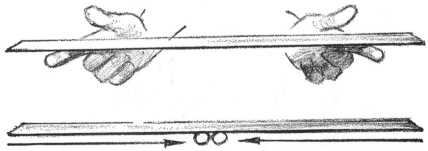

PARADOX ON WHEELS

Which goes faster, the top or bottom of a rolling wheel?

The question is tricky, because it isn't clear exactly what is meant by "top" or "bottom." Nevertheless, there is a sense in which one can say that the top of a rolling wheel moves faster than the bottom. In the sketch below, the wheel has made one quarter-turn as it rolls to the right. Note that top point T has traveled much farther to reach T^1 than bottom point B has traveled to reach B^1. Since these distances are traversed in the same time period, point T must have gone faster than point B.

In other words, parts of the wheel that for the time being are the upper half move faster than parts that momentarily form the lower half. This is why, if you look through a rolling wheel with spokes, it is easier to distinguish the slower-moving spokes in the lower half than it is to see those in the upper half.

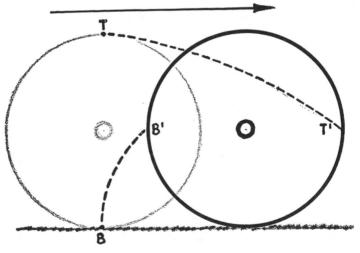

MAKE A BOOMERANG

Cut a small L-shaped boomerang from a piece of heavy cardboard. The exact shape and size do not matter, but the ends should be rounded as shown. Rest it on a book, tipping the book toward you. Then strike the projecting end sharply with a pencil. The boomerang will whirl forward and up, then glide back toward you along the same path. You may have to practice a few times to get the knack.

The spin of the boomerang is essential to its working, because it converts the cardboard into a gyroscope. As long as it spins it will maintain the same plane of rotation. When it falls, the force of air on the rotating and inclined blades pushes the boomerang back toward you.

THE UNBREAKABLE MATCH

Hold a wooden kitchen match with the tips of your fingers, as shown. Try to break it. You'll be surprised to find that it can't be done.

This is easily understood when you realize that the muscles of the hand move the fingers in the manner of a third-class lever. Such a lever is one that has the fulcrum (F) at one end, the resistance (R) at the other end, and the effort (E) applied somewhere in between. Tweezers and sugar tongs are common examples.

This type of lever sacrifices power for a wider arc of movement at the resistance end. The longer the distance from the resistance (in this case, the match) to the fulcrum (base of finger) as compared to the distance from the effort (where the muscle is attached) to the fulcrum, the less the "mechanical advantage" of the lever. If you slide the match closer to the base of the fingers, the mechanical advantage increases enormously. Then the match can be easily snapped.

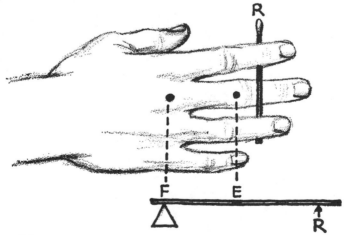

A popular trick among Hindu fakirs is that of plunging a dagger into a bowl of rice. When the fakir lifts the dagger, the bowl is raised with it. Oddly enough, there is no "gimmick." You can do the trick yourself with a glass jar, a box of uncooked rice, and a knife.

The jar must be wider than its opening. Fill it to the brim with rice, packing the grains down with your thumbs. Plunge the knife straight down into the rice. Pull it out and repeat, in a series of quick jabs no more than a few inches deep. With each stab, the grains pack more tightly. After a dozen or more of these short jabs, plunge the knife down as far as you can. If enough chains of rice grains wedge themselves against the blade and the top of the jar, you can lift the knife, and the entire jar will cling mysteriously to it!

PENNY POSER

Arrange three pennies on a smooth surface, as shown. Challenge anyone to move penny C to a position between pennies A and B, while observing the following conditions: B must not be moved from its position, and A must not be touched in any way.

Few people are likely to hit on the method, unless they recall that solid bodies are capable of transmitting a force without moving. Simply place the tip of your left forefinger firmly on top of B. Slide C toward it, releasing the penny before it strikes the right edge of B. The force of the blow will be transmitted to A, shooting it off to the left. You now have only to put C between the other two coins, and the trick is done.

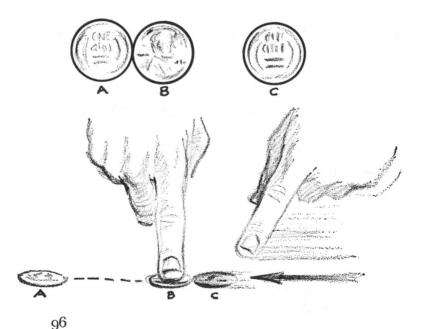

MATCHBOX STABILIZER

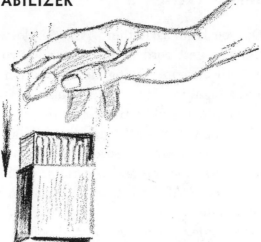

Challenge someone to hold a box of matches (the type with a sliding drawer) a foot above the table, then drop it so it lands on one end and remains standing. When he tries it, the box will bounce and land on its side.

The trick is to take advantage of the stabilizing power of momentum (speed times mass). Push the drawer about an inch out of the cover, then drop the box, as shown. When it hits the table, the momentum of the drawer sliding shut will prevent the box from falling over. Gyroscope stabilizers in airplanes, torpedoes, and guided missiles operate on the same basic principle. The only difference is that, in these, the momentum is created by rapidly spinning wheels.

The ordinary housefly has a pair of stabilizers that consist of a vibrating rod under each wing, with a tiny ball-weight on the tip of each rod. When these halters (as they are called) are cut off, the fly loses all control of his balance during flight.

97

SUPER-STRENGTH

Do you know that there is a simple way to break even the strongest cord or fish line with your bare hands? It is both an entertaining demonstration of super-strength and a highly useful thing to know.

Wrap one end of the cord around your left forefinger, then loop it around the hand exactly as shown. With your other hand, seize the cord a foot or two below, wrapping it several times around the right hand. Close both hands into fists. Hold the fists close together, then quickly yank your right fist down and your left fist up. The cord will snap inside your left fist at the point marked A.

The feat illustrates the fact that pressure is the force divided by the area on which the force operates. By looping the cord as shown, the force is concentrated on the tiny area where the cord intersects itself. This raises the pressure enough so that the cord acts like a dull knife blade and literally cuts through itself.

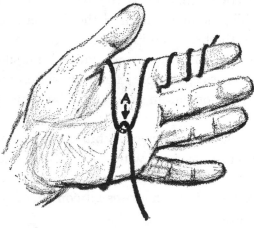

POTATO PUNCTURE

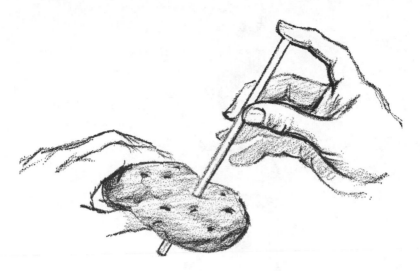

Can a soda straw, held like a small spear, be plunged completely through an unpeeled potato? It seem impossible, but it isn't. Hold the potato and straw exactly as shown. Your forefinger should cover the top opening of the straw. Then, as you move your hand downward, a column of air will be trapped in the straw, keeping it rigid.

Strike the potato quickly, with as much force as you can. Be sure the straw is perpendicular to the surface of the potato when it hits. Otherwise the straw will tend to crumple.

It may take a bit of experimenting to get the knack. But once you master it, you can puncture the potato almost every time. After a successful spearing, you'll find a neat little potato cylinder tucked tightly inside the end of the straw.

There is perhaps no more dramatic way of demonstrating the effects of air pressure than this stunt of putting a hard-boiled egg into a glass milk bottle and getting it out intact.

Remove the shell, stand the egg on the bottle's mouth, and challenge your spectators to push it inside the bottle. They'll find it impossible. Since the air in the bottle has no outlet, it will firmly resist any pressure on the egg.

You show how it can be done by dropping a burning match into the bottle just before you put the egg on the mouth. When the flame goes out, the air cools and contracts, forming a vacuum that draws the egg inside.

How do you get it out again? After everyone has tried and failed, turn the bottle upside down so the egg falls into the neck. Tip back your head and blow vigorously into the inverted bottle as shown.

When you remove your lips, the egg will pop out so quickly that you'll be wise to keep your other hand near the opening so you can catch it.

DANCING DIME

The next time you enjoy a soft drink, give this entertaining science stunt a try. When the bottle is empty but still cold, put a dime on the opening as shown. Dip your finger in water and let a drop or two fall around the edge of the dime to seal the opening.

Now place both hands around the bottle, holding it firmly for about fifteen seconds. The dime will start to click up and down mysteriously. Let it dance for a while, then remove your hands. The dime goes right on clicking!

The trick is a simple illustration of how air expands when heated. The cold air inside the bottle is warmed by the heat from your palms. The expanding air escapes around the rim of the dime, causing it to flutter.

102

THE MAGDEBURG
TUMBLERS

In Magdeburg, Germany, in 1650, a famous experiment was performed with two hollow iron hemispheres. They were placed together and the air removed from their insides. This created a vacuum so strong that it required eight teams of horses to pull the hemispheres apart.

The experiment can be demonstrated on a smaller scale by means of two glasses and a piece of blotting paper dipped in water. Light several matches and drop them into one tumbler. Put the wet blotting paper on the brim, then quickly invert the second glass on the paper as shown.

The porous paper allows the partial vacuum, caused by the cooling and contracting air, to fill both glasses. When you lift the top glass, the paper and the bottom glass will come with it!

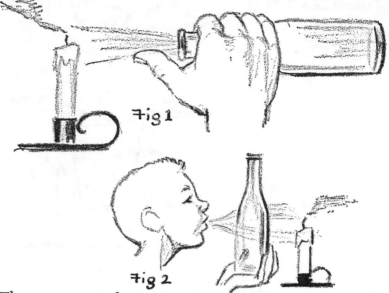

Fig 1

Fig 2

There are several amusing ways to blow out a candle, all of them having scientific interest. For example: Put your thumb over the opening of an empty soda bottle; then put your mouth over both opening and thumb. Lift your thumb, blow as hard as you can, and trap the compressed air by again closing the opening with your thumb. Now, if you aim the bottle at a candle flame (Fig. 1) and quickly remove your thumb, the bottle will obligingly puff out the flame.

Light the candle again, hold the bottle between your mouth and the flame (Fig. 2), and blow. The flame will go out just as though you were blowing straight through the bottle. What happens is that the air moving past the bottle creates a partial vacuum behind the bottle, and the air that rushes in to fill the vacuum puts out the flame.

THE FLOATING BALL

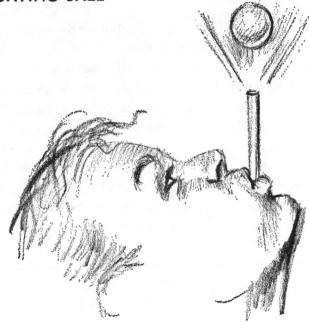

Snip a six-inch piece from the end of a soda straw. Put one end of the piece on your mouth, tip back your head, and hold a table-tennis ball a few inches above the other end. Blow as hard as you can, simultaneously releasing the ball. Instead of being blown away as you might expect, it remains suspended in mid-air. The harder you blow, the higher it floats above the straw.

The explanation: when air is in rapid motion, its pressure is lowered. In this trick, the ball is actually imprisoned by the column of upward rushing air. As soon as it wobbles a bit to one side, the greater pressure outside the "jet stream" forces the ball back into it again.

SMOKE RINGS

By folding the ends of six playing cards (or file cards) and fitting them together as shown, you can produce a neat little cubical box. Cut a small round hole in the center of one card. Ask Dad to take a puff on his cigar, pipe, or cigarette and gently blow the smoke into the box. Now, if you tap the side of the box, a perfect smoke ring will rise from the opening.

The stunt should be performed in a room free of air currents. When the box is tapped rapidly, a series of rings will emerge and expand in time to the tapping, creating a novel and entertaining spectacle.

BOILING WITHOUT HEAT

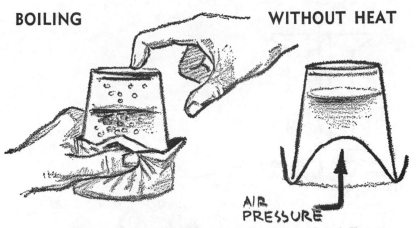

AIR PRESSURE

Years ago I saw a gypsy woman perform the following feat as a demonstration of her supposedly magic powers. She filled a drinking glass with water, then covered it with her handkerchief, previously dipped in water. She pushed down the center of the cloth to form a kind of well, inverted the glass on her right palm, then seized it with her left hand as shown. Air pressure ballooned the cloth upward inside the glass.

"When I put my finger on the glass," she explained, "it will make the water boil." Sure enough, when she did so, streams of bubbles began rising through the water. You could even *hear* the surface bubbling!

What happened was this. When she pushed with her finger, the glass slid downward through her left hand, causing the handkerchief to slide upward on the outside of the glass. This lowered the center of the cloth inside, forming a vacuum. The vacuum drew air through the handkerchief's cloth fibers and created a perfect illusion of boiling water.

(Note: Be sure to do your practicing over the sink.)

107

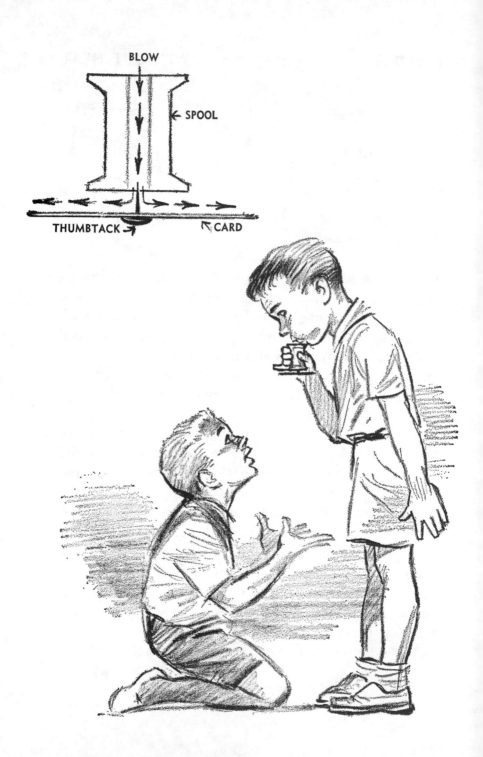

BLOW

SPOOL

THUMBTACK

CARD

BERNOULLI'S PRINCIPLE

Push a thumbtack through the center of a playing card and place a spool over the point of the tack as shown. Holding the spool in one hand and the card in the other, put your lips to the spool and blow down through it as hard as you can. At the same time, release the card.

You would expect the card to be blown to the floor. Actually, it clings to the spool as long as you blow.

The explanation lies in what is known as "Bernoulli's principle" (named after Daniel Bernoulli, an eighteenth-century Swiss scientist). This principle states that when a gas or liquid is in motion, its pressure is reduced; the more rapid the motion, the greater the reduction in pressure. Blowing into the spool causes air to flow rapidly over the top of the card, lowering the air pressure. The stronger air pressure below the card keeps it from falling.

This is exactly what happens when an airplane moves forward. The wings are so designed that air rushes across their upper surfaces at a faster rate than it rushes past the lower surfaces. Thanks to Bernoulli's principle, this lowers the pressure more above the wings than below, producing the lifting force that sustains the heavy plane in the air.

The magician drops a shirt button into a glass filled with a carbonated beverage. It sinks to the bottom. A moment or two later, he waves his hand over the glass and says, "Button, rise!" The button floats slowly to the surface. When the magician snaps his fingers and says, "Button, sink!" down it goes again.

This startling trick works automatically with any small light object. While it's resting on the bottom of the glass, tiny bubbles of carbon dioxide begin to cluster around it. When enough bubbles have collected to counteract the object's weight, they float it to the surface. On the surface, the bubbles burst and the weight of the object carries it down again. This up and down motion continues as long as there is carbonation in the liquid.

The magician, of course, has experimented beforehand with his button so that he knows just how long to wait each time before he issues a command.

SELF-STARTING SIPHON

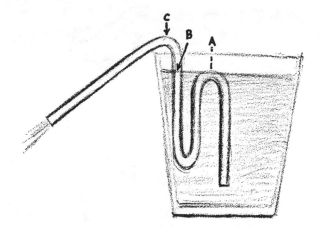

Many strange types of self-starting siphons have been invented, but this one is so elementary that you can construct it yourself from a single piece of glass tubing.

With the aid of a Bunsen burner, bend the tube into the shape indicated in the drawing. Allow it to cool. When the bent part is submerged in water as shown, the siphon will immediately start flowing.

This is what happens. As soon as point A on the tube goes beneath the surface, the water (seeking its own level) rushes through the tube to fill it to point B. Due to its inertia, however, the moving water is carried up and over bend C to start the siphon.

The siphon can also be made with Flex-straws, a type of soda straw currently on the market. These straws are so prepared that they can be bent without impeding the flow of liquid through them. Three such straws, cut to the proper lengths, can be joined with cellophane tape to make the siphon.

Pascal's law tells us that pressure applied to a confined liquid is transmitted undiminished to all parts of the liquid. This can be demonstrated with an empty soda bottle, a few paper book matches, and a toy balloon.

Remove the heads of the matches and then drop the heads into the bottle. Fill the bottle to the brim with water and fasten the mouth of the balloon tightly over the bottle's opening. The match heads will float on top of the water, but when you press your finger on the balloon diaphragm they will sink slowly to the bottom. Remove your finger, and the heads float up again.

The explanation is this. The pressure is transmitted through the water, forcing a tiny amount of liquid to penetrate the porous paper edge of each match head. This adds enough weight to the match head to make it sink. When you remove your finger, there is enough air pressure inside the heads to force out the water, so up they go.

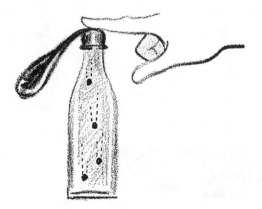

BRIM TO BRIM

Stand two glasses completely filled with water, brim to brim inside a cereal bowl, as shown. Move the upper glass a trifle to make a tiny, barely perceptible opening between the rims. Surface tension and the air pressure outside the glasses will prevent the water from escaping. Can you remove the water from the upper glass without touching either glass in any way?

The feat can be accomplished with a soda straw. Hold one end close to the opening between the brims and blow through the other. Air will bubble up into the top glass, forcing water out through the opening and down into the bowl.

(If, by the way, you have any trouble with the first part of the trick—getting the two full glasses brim to brim —just plunge them underwater in a sink, put them together, and lift out.)

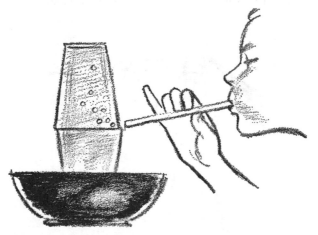

Dip a woman's handkerchief in water and wring it out. Then twist it like a rope, and hang it over the brims of two glasses arranged as shown. Be sure that the handkerchief touches the bottom of the higher glass, but hangs only a short distance below the rim of the lower one. Fill the top glass with water, and go away. By the next morning, you should find all the water in the lower glass.

The handkerchief, of course, is not a true siphon. The water is drawn through the cloth by capillary attraction— the tendency of liquids to rise in thin-bore tubes and move through porous materials such as cloth and blotting paper.

TWO-TONE CORSAGE

Capillary action carries water from the soil up through the roots of plants and trees, through the trunk or stem, and into the flowers and leaves. The liquid rises through sap tubes that are tiny enough to produce the required capillary force. The process is easily demonstrated by this simple experiment.

Fill two glasses with water. Color the water in one glass red by using Easter-egg dye or food coloring. Carefully split the stem of a white carnation (any other white flower will also do). Place half the stem in one glass, the other half in the other glass, as shown. After a few hours you will find that one side of the blossom has turned a beautiful crimson.

Worn by a young lady as a corsage, this two-toned carnation is sure to attract attention and serve as a conversation starter.

Fill a drinking glass with enough water to reach almost to the rim. Drop a small cork into the glass, and challenge anyone to make the cork float in the center of the water without touching the sides of the glass. He'll find it impossible. The cork always drifts to one side.

After everyone gives up, show how easily it can be done. Add more water to the glass, pouring carefully from another glass until the water rises slightly above the rim. Because of surface tension, the water will form a convex surface, as shown. The cork naturally moves to the center, where the water is highest, and there it will remain.

HEAT

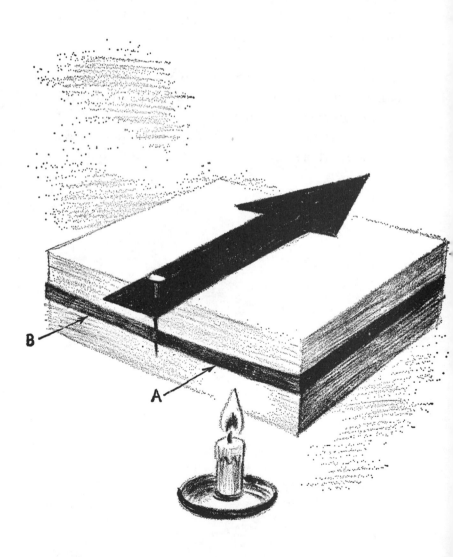

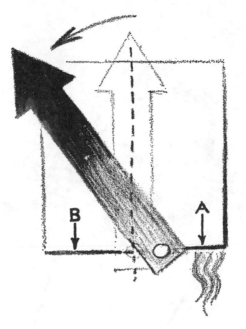

Unlike most substances, rubber contracts when heated, expands when cooled. This can be demonstrated by the following experiment.

Stretch a rubber band around the sides of a box. Cut out a cardboard arrow, mount it on a pin, and push the pin under the band as shown. If you now bring a burning match or candle close to segment A of the band, the cardboard arrow will rotate slowly counterclockwise. Move the flame near segment B and the arrow rotates clockwise. The heat, of course, causes a portion of the band to contract, rotating the pin to which the arrow is attached.

119

SOUND

Tie the hook of a wire coat hanger to the center of a piece of string about five feet long. Wrap one end of the string several times around your left index finger; then wrap the other end the same way around your right index finger. Push the tips of both fingers into your ears.

Now bend forward and allow the hanger to strike against the side of a chair as shown. You'll be startled to hear a sound like the chiming of an old-fashioned clock or a church bell tolling in the distance.

The tone is produced, of course, by the vibrations of the hanger. The sound waves are then transmitted to your eardrums via string and fingers.

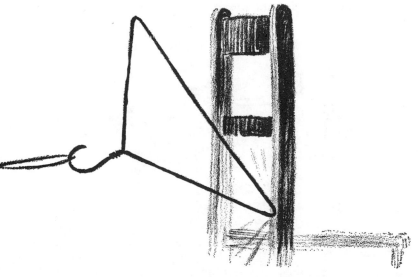

FRANKLIN'S ARMONICA

One of Benjamin Franklin's many curious inventions was a musical instrument he called an "armonica." Foot pedals rotated a series of glass bowls of graduated sizes, all kept moist by a trough of water in which the lower parts of each bowl were submerged. When a finger was touched to a spinning bowl, a clear musical tone resulted.

The principle of the armonica is easily demonstrated with a glass of water. (Thin glasses work best.) Dip the end of your middle finger in the water, and run the moist finger tip slowly around the rim of the glass, as shown. The finger must be neither too wet nor too dry, so be patient and keep trying until you hear a strong, clear tone coming from the glass.

Actually, your finger moves around the rim in a series of tiny jerks. It slips, catches, slips, and catches. These imperceptible movements make the glass vibrate and produce a tone, just as a violin bow, by similar frictional movements, causes a catgut string to produce a tone.

If you pluck one of the inside prongs of a fork with a table knife as shown, you will hear nothing. But if you immediately press the end of the fork's handle against a table top, you will hear a distinct tone.

This is the basis of a delightful after-dinner trick, although it will take some practice. First, pluck the fork; then hold the blade of the knife over an empty glass. At the instant the knife is above the glass, your other hand slyly allows the end of the fork to come in contact with the table. Everyone will be watching the knife and will assume that the sound is coming from the glass. But when they try the trick, it won't work.

The tone actually comes from the table, which picks up and amplifies the fork's vibrations. Physicists call the phenomenon "sympathetic vibration."

INERTIA

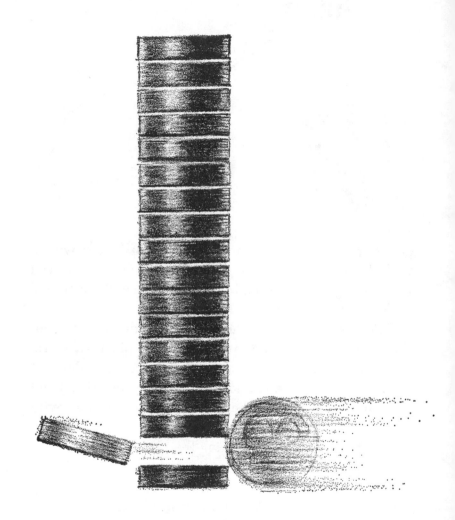

Form a tower of black checkers with one red checker second from the bottom. A foot away, stand another checker on edge as shown. If you press your finger down on the edge of this checker, you can shoot it forward toward the stack. It will strike the stack and knock out the one red checker without toppling the others.

The stunt is a neat demonstration of inertia, for it is the inertia of the black checkers that keeps them in place while the red checker is sliding out. (If the checkers you use are thinner than most, you may find that the red checker will have to be placed third from the bottom instead of second.)

THE EGG AND I-NERTIA

Let's suppose someone presented you with a dozen eggs on a plate and said, "One of these eggs is hard-boiled. The rest are raw. Can you find the hard-boiled egg without cracking any shells?"

You could, by utilizing the laws of inertia. Clear the plate; then try to spin each egg on the plate. The only egg that will spin readily is the hard-boiled one. With a raw egg, the inertia of its liquid exerts a drag effect that kills the spin.

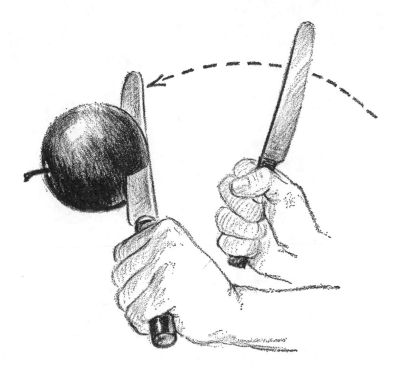

Force the blade of a table knife into an apple just far enough to make the apple stick to the knife when you hold it as shown. Now rap the end of the knife sharply with the back of another table knife, striking as close to the fruit as possible. Inertia prevents the apple from moving as quickly as the knife that is struck. This causes the blade to slice the fruit neatly in two.

127

A CATALOG OF
SELECTED DOVER BOOKS
IN ALL FIELDS OF INTEREST

A CATALOG OF SELECTED DOVER BOOKS IN ALL FIELDS OF INTEREST

CONCERNING THE SPIRITUAL IN ART, Wassily Kandinsky. Pioneering work by father of abstract art. Thoughts on color theory, nature of art. Analysis of earlier masters. 12 illustrations. 80pp. of text. 5⅜ × 8½. 23411-8 Pa. $2.25

LEONARDO ON THE HUMAN BODY, Leonardo da Vinci. More than 1200 of Leonardo's anatomical drawings on 215 plates. Leonardo's text, which accompanies the drawings, has been translated into English. 506pp. 8⅜ × 11¾. 24483-0 Pa. $10.95

GOBLIN MARKET, Christina Rossetti. Best-known work by poet comparable to Emily Dickinson, Alfred Tennyson. With 46 delightfully grotesque illustrations by Laurence Housman. 64pp. 4 × 6¾. 24516-0 Pa. $2.50

THE HEART OF THOREAU'S JOURNALS, edited by Odell Shepard. Selections from *Journal*, ranging over full gamut of interests. 228pp. 5⅜ × 8½. 20741-2 Pa. $4.00

MR. LINCOLN'S CAMERA MAN: MATHEW B. BRADY, Roy Meredith. Over 300 Brady photos reproduced directly from original negatives, photos. Lively commentary. 368pp. 8⅜ × 11¼. 23021-X Pa. $11.95

PHOTOGRAPHIC VIEWS OF SHERMAN'S CAMPAIGN, George N. Barnard. Reprint of landmark 1866 volume with 61 plates: battlefield of New Hope Church, the Etawah Bridge, the capture of Atlanta, etc. 80pp. 9 × 12. 23445-2 Pa. $6.00

A SHORT HISTORY OF ANATOMY AND PHYSIOLOGY FROM THE GREEKS TO HARVEY, Dr. Charles Singer. Thoroughly engrossing non-technical survey. 270 illustrations. 211pp. 5⅜ × 8½. 20389-1 Pa. $4.50

REDOUTE ROSES IRON-ON TRANSFER PATTERNS, Barbara Christopher. Redouté was botanical painter to the Empress Josephine; transfer his famous roses onto fabric with these 24 transfer patterns. 80pp. 8¼ × 10⅞. 24292-7 Pa. $3.50

THE FIVE BOOKS OF ARCHITECTURE, Sebastiano Serlio. Architectural milestone, first (1611) English translation of Renaissance classic. Unabridged reproduction of original edition includes over 300 woodcut illustrations. 416pp. 9⅜ × 12¼. 24349-4 Pa. $14.95

CARLSON'S GUIDE TO LANDSCAPE PAINTING, John F. Carlson. Authoritative, comprehensive guide covers, every aspect of landscape painting. 34 reproductions of paintings by author; 58 explanatory diagrams. 144pp. 8⅜ × 11. 22927-0 Pa. $4.95

101 PUZZLES IN THOUGHT AND LOGIC, C.R. Wylie, Jr. Solve murders, robberies, see which fishermen are liars—purely by reasoning! 107pp. 5⅜ × 8½. 20367-0 Pa. $2.00

TEST YOUR LOGIC, George J. Summers. 50 more truly new puzzles with new turns of thought, new subtleties of inference. 100pp. 5⅜ × 8½. 22877-0 Pa. $2.25

THE MURDER BOOK OF J.G. REEDER, Edgar Wallace. Eight suspenseful stories by bestselling mystery writer of 20s and 30s. Features the donnish Mr. J.G. Reeder of Public Prosecutor's Office. 128pp. 5⅜ × 8½. (Available in U.S. only)
24374-5 Pa. $3.50

ANNE ORR'S CHARTED DESIGNS, Anne Orr. Best designs by premier needlework designer, all on charts: flowers, borders, birds, children, alphabets, etc. Over 100 charts, 10 in color. Total of 40pp. 8¼ × 11. 23704-4 Pa. $2.25

BASIC CONSTRUCTION TECHNIQUES FOR HOUSES AND SMALL BUILDINGS SIMPLY EXPLAINED, U.S. Bureau of Naval Personnel. Grading, masonry, woodworking, floor and wall framing, roof framing, plastering, tile setting, much more. Over 675 illustrations. 568pp. 6½ × 9¼. 20242-9 Pa. $8.95

MATISSE LINE DRAWINGS AND PRINTS, Henri Matisse. Representative collection of female nudes, faces, still lifes, experimental works, etc., from 1898 to 1948. 50 illustrations. 48pp. 8⅜ × 11¼. 23877-6 Pa. $2.50

HOW TO PLAY THE CHESS OPENINGS, Eugene Znosko-Borovsky. Clear, profound examinations of just what each opening is intended to do and how opponent can counter. Many sample games. 147pp. 5⅜ × 8½. 22795-2 Pa. $2.95

DUPLICATE BRIDGE, Alfred Sheinwold. Clear, thorough, easily followed account: rules, etiquette, scoring, strategy, bidding; Goren's point-count system, Blackwood and Gerber conventions, etc. 158pp. 5⅜ × 8½. 22741-3 Pa. $3.00

SARGENT PORTRAIT DRAWINGS, J.S. Sargent. Collection of 42 portraits reveals technical skill and intuitive eye of noted American portrait painter, John Singer Sargent. 48pp. 8¼ × 11⅛. 24524-1 Pa. $2.95

ENTERTAINING SCIENCE EXPERIMENTS WITH EVERYDAY OBJECTS, Martin Gardner. Over 100 experiments for youngsters. Will amuse, astonish, teach, and entertain. Over 100 illustrations. 127pp. 5⅜ × 8½. 24201-3 Pa. $2.50

TEDDY BEAR PAPER DOLLS IN FULL COLOR: A Family of Four Bears and Their Costumes, Crystal Collins. A family of four Teddy Bear paper dolls and nearly 60 cut-out costumes. Full color, printed one side only. 32pp. 9¼ × 12¼.
24550-0 Pa. $3.50

NEW CALLIGRAPHIC ORNAMENTS AND FLOURISHES, Arthur Baker. Unusual, multi-useable material: arrows, pointing hands, brackets and frames, ovals, swirls, birds, etc. Nearly 700 illustrations. 80pp. 8⅜ × 11¼.
24095-9 Pa. $3.50

DINOSAUR DIORAMAS TO CUT & ASSEMBLE, M. Kalmenoff. Two complete three-dimensional scenes in full color, with 31 cut-out animals and plants. Excellent educational toy for youngsters. Instructions; 2 assembly diagrams. 32pp. 9¼ × 12¼. 24541-1 Pa. $3.95

SILHOUETTES: A PICTORIAL ARCHIVE OF VARIED ILLUSTRATIONS, edited by Carol Belanger Grafton. Over 600 silhouettes from the 18th to 20th centuries. Profiles and full figures of men, women, children, birds, animals, groups and scenes, nature, ships, an alphabet. 144pp. 8⅜ × 11¼. 23781-8 Pa. $4.50

25 KITES THAT FLY, Leslie Hunt. Full, easy-to-follow instructions for kites made from inexpensive materials. Many novelties. 70 illustrations. 110pp. 5⅜ × 8½.
22550-X Pa. $1.95

PIANO TUNING, J. Cree Fischer. Clearest, best book for beginner, amateur. Simple repairs, raising dropped notes, tuning by easy method of flattened fifths. No previous skills needed. 4 illustrations. 201pp. 5⅜ × 8½.
23267-0 Pa. $3.50

EARLY AMERICAN IRON-ON TRANSFER PATTERNS, edited by Rita Weiss. 75 designs, borders, alphabets, from traditional American sources. 48pp. 8¼ × 11.
23162-3 Pa. $1.95

CROCHETING EDGINGS, edited by Rita Weiss. Over 100 of the best designs for these lovely trims for a host of household items. Complete instructions, illustrations. 48pp. 8¼ × 11.
24031-2 Pa. $2.00

FINGER PLAYS FOR NURSERY AND KINDERGARTEN, Emilie Poulsson. 18 finger plays with music (voice and piano); entertaining, instructive. Counting, nature lore, etc. Victorian classic. 53 illustrations. 80pp. 6½ × 9¼. 22588-7 Pa. $1.95

BOSTON THEN AND NOW, Peter Vanderwarker. Here in 59 side-by-side views are photographic documentations of the city's past and present. 119 photographs. Full captions. 122pp. 8¼ × 11.
24312-5 Pa. $6.95

CROCHETING BEDSPREADS, edited by Rita Weiss. 22 patterns, originally published in three instruction books 1939-41. 39 photos, 8 charts. Instructions. 48pp. 8¼ × 11.
23610-2 Pa. $2.00

HAWTHORNE ON PAINTING, Charles W. Hawthorne. Collected from notes taken by students at famous Cape Cod School; hundreds of direct, personal *apercus*, ideas, suggestions. 91pp. 5⅜ × 8½.
20653-X Pa. $2.50

THERMODYNAMICS, Enrico Fermi. A classic of modern science. Clear, organized treatment of systems, first and second laws, entropy, thermodynamic potentials, etc. Calculus required. 160pp. 5⅜ × 8½.
60361-X Pa. $4.00

TEN BOOKS ON ARCHITECTURE, Vitruvius. The most important book ever written on architecture. Early Roman aesthetics, technology, classical orders, site selection, all other aspects. Morgan translation. 331pp. 5⅜ × 8½. 20645-9 Pa. $5.50

THE CORNELL BREAD BOOK, Clive M. McCay and Jeanette B. McCay. Famed high-protein recipe incorporated into breads, rolls, buns, coffee cakes, pizza, pie crusts, more. Nearly 50 illustrations. 48pp. 8¼ × 11.
23995-0 Pa. $2.00

THE CRAFTSMAN'S HANDBOOK, Cennino Cennini. 15th-century handbook, school of Giotto, explains applying gold, silver leaf; gesso; fresco painting, grinding pigments, etc. 142pp. 6⅛ × 9¼.
20054-X Pa. $3.50

FRANK LLOYD WRIGHT'S FALLINGWATER, Donald Hoffmann. Full story of Wright's masterwork at Bear Run, Pa. 100 photographs of site, construction, and details of completed structure. 112pp. 9¼ × 10.
23671-4 Pa. $6.50

OVAL STAINED GLASS PATTERN BOOK, C. Eaton. 60 new designs framed in shape of an oval. Greater complexity, challenge with sinuous cats, birds, mandalas framed in antique shape. 64pp. 8¼ × 11.
24519-5 Pa. $3.50

THE BOOK OF WOOD CARVING, Charles Marshall Sayers. Still finest book for beginning student. Fundamentals, technique; gives 34 designs, over 34 projects for panels, bookends, mirrors, etc. 33 photos. 118pp. 7¾ × 10⅝.   23654-4 Pa. $3.95

CARVING COUNTRY CHARACTERS, Bill Higginbotham. Expert advice for beginning, advanced carvers on materials, techniques for creating 18 projects—mirthful panorama of American characters. 105 illustrations. 80pp. 8⅜ × 11.
24135-1 Pa. $2.50

300 ART NOUVEAU DESIGNS AND MOTIFS IN FULL COLOR, C.B. Grafton. 44 full-page plates display swirling lines and muted colors typical of Art Nouveau. Borders, frames, panels, cartouches, dingbats, etc. 48pp. 9⅜ × 12¼.
24354-0 Pa. $6.00

SELF-WORKING CARD TRICKS, Karl Fulves. Editor of *Pallbearer* offers 72 tricks that work automatically through nature of card deck. No sleight of hand needed. Often spectacular. 42 illustrations. 113pp. 5⅜ × 8½.   23334-0 Pa. $2.25

CUT AND ASSEMBLE A WESTERN FRONTIER TOWN, Edmund V. Gillon, Jr. Ten authentic full-color buildings on heavy cardboard stock in H-O scale. Sheriff's Office and Jail, Saloon, Wells Fargo, Opera House, others. 48pp. 9¼ × 12¼.
23736-2 Pa. $3.95

CUT AND ASSEMBLE AN EARLY NEW ENGLAND VILLAGE, Edmund V. Gillon, Jr. Printed in full color on heavy cardboard stock. 12 authentic buildings in H-O scale: Adams home in Quincy, Mass., Oliver Wight house in Sturbridge, smithy, store, church, others. 48pp. 9¼ × 12¼.   23536-X Pa. $3.95

THE TALE OF TWO BAD MICE, Beatrix Potter. Tom Thumb and Hunca Munca squeeze out of their hole and go exploring. 27 full-color Potter illustrations. 59pp. 4¼ × 5½. (Available in U.S. only)   23065-1 Pa. $1.50

CARVING FIGURE CARICATURES IN THE OZARK STYLE, Harold L. Enlow. Instructions and illustrations for ten delightful projects, plus general carving instructions. 22 drawings and 47 photographs altogether. 39pp. 8⅜ × 11.
23151-8 Pa. $2.50

A TREASURY OF FLOWER DESIGNS FOR ARTISTS, EMBROIDERERS AND CRAFTSMEN, Susan Gaber. 100 garden favorites lushly rendered by artist for artists, craftsmen, needleworkers. Many form frames, borders. 80pp. 8¼ × 11.
24096-7 Pa. $3.50

CUT & ASSEMBLE A TOY THEATER/THE NUTCRACKER BALLET, Tom Tierney. Model of a complete, full-color production of Tchaikovsky's classic. 6 backdrops, dozens of characters, familiar dance sequences. 32pp. 9⅜ × 12¼.
24194-7 Pa. $4.50

ANIMALS: 1,419 COPYRIGHT-FREE ILLUSTRATIONS OF MAMMALS, BIRDS, FISH, INSECTS, ETC., edited by Jim Harter. Clear wood engravings present, in extremely lifelike poses, over 1,000 species of animals. 284pp. 9 × 12.
23766-4 Pa. $8.95

MORE HAND SHADOWS, Henry Bursill. For those at their 'finger ends,'' 16 more effects—Shakespeare, a hare, a squirrel, Mr. Punch, and twelve more—each explained by a full-page illustration. Considerable period charm. 30pp. 6½ × 9¼.
21384-6 Pa. $1.95

SURREAL STICKERS AND UNREAL STAMPS, William Rowe. 224 haunting, hilarious stamps on gummed, perforated stock, with images of elephants, geisha girls, George Washington, etc. 16pp. one side. 8¼ × 11. 24371-0 Pa. $3.50

GOURMET KITCHEN LABELS, Ed Sibbett, Jr. 112 full-color labels (4 copies each of 28 designs). Fruit, bread, other culinary motifs. Gummed and perforated. 16pp. 8¼ × 11. 24087-8 Pa. $2.95

PATTERNS AND INSTRUCTIONS FOR CARVING AUTHENTIC BIRDS, H.D. Green. Detailed instructions, 27 diagrams, 85 photographs for carving 15 species of birds so life-like, they'll seem ready to fly! 8¼ × 11. 24222-6 Pa. $2.75

FLATLAND, E.A. Abbott. Science-fiction classic explores life of 2-D being in 3-D world. 16 illustrations. 103pp. 5⅜ × 8. 20001-9 Pa. $2.00

DRIED FLOWERS, Sarah Whitlock and Martha Rankin. Concise, clear, practical guide to dehydration, glycerinizing, pressing plant material, and more. Covers use of silica gel. 12 drawings. 32pp. 5⅜ × 8½. 21802-3 Pa. $1.00

EASY-TO-MAKE CANDLES, Gary V. Guy. Learn how easy it is to make all kinds of decorative candles. Step-by-step instructions. 82 illustrations. 48pp. 8¼ × 11. 23881-4 Pa. $2.50

SUPER STICKERS FOR KIDS, Carolyn Bracken. 128 gummed and perforated full-color stickers: GIRL WANTED, KEEP OUT, BORED OF EDUCATION, X-RATED, COMBAT ZONE, many others. 16pp. 8¼ × 11. 24092-4 Pa. $2.50

CUT AND COLOR PAPER MASKS, Michael Grater. Clowns, animals, funny faces...simply color them in, cut them out, and put them together, and you have 9 paper masks to play with and enjoy. 32pp. 8¼ × 11. 23171-2 Pa. $2.25

A CHRISTMAS CAROL: THE ORIGINAL MANUSCRIPT, Charles Dickens. Clear facsimile of Dickens manuscript, on facing pages with final printed text. 8 illustrations by John Leech, 4 in color on covers. 144pp. 8⅜ × 11¼. 20980-6 Pa. $5.95

CARVING SHOREBIRDS, Harry V. Shourds & Anthony Hillman. 16 full-size patterns (all double-page spreads) for 19 North American shorebirds with step-by-step instructions. 72pp. 9¼ × 12¼. 24287-0 Pa. $4.95

THE GENTLE ART OF MATHEMATICS, Dan Pedoe. Mathematical games, probability, the question of infinity, topology, how the laws of algebra work, problems of irrational numbers, and more. 42 figures. 143pp. 5⅜ × 8½. (EBE) 22949-1 Pa. $3.00

READY-TO-USE DOLLHOUSE WALLPAPER, Katzenbach & Warren, Inc. Stripe, 2 floral stripes, 2 allover florals, polka dot; all in full color. 4 sheets (350 sq. in.) of each, enough for average room. 48pp. 8¼ × 11. 23495-9 Pa. $2.95

MINIATURE IRON-ON TRANSFER PATTERNS FOR DOLLHOUSES, DOLLS, AND SMALL PROJECTS, Rita Weiss and Frank Fontana. Over 100 miniature patterns: rugs, bedspreads, quilts, chair seats, etc. In standard dollhouse size. 48pp. 8¼ × 11. 23741-9 Pa. $1.95

THE DINOSAUR COLORING BOOK, Anthony Rao. 45 renderings of dinosaurs, fossil birds, turtles, other creatures of Mesozoic Era. Scientifically accurate. Captions. 48pp. 8¼ × 11. 24022-3 Pa. $2.25

JAPANESE DESIGN MOTIFS, Matsuya Co. Mon, or heraldic designs. Over 4000 typical, beautiful designs: birds, animals, flowers, swords, fans, geometrics; all beautifully stylized. 213pp. 11⅜ × 8¼. 22874-6 Pa. $6.95

THE TALE OF BENJAMIN BUNNY, Beatrix Potter. Peter Rabbit's cousin coaxes him back into Mr. McGregor's garden for a whole new set of adventures. All 27 full-color illustrations. 59pp. 4¼ × 5½. (Available in U.S. only) 21102-9 Pa. $1.50

THE TALE OF PETER RABBIT AND OTHER FAVORITE STORIES BOXED SET, Beatrix Potter. Seven of Beatrix Potter's best-loved tales including Peter Rabbit in a specially designed, durable boxed set. 4¼ × 5½. Total of 447pp. 158 color illustrations. (Available in U.S. only) 23903-9 Pa. $10.50

PRACTICAL MENTAL MAGIC, Theodore Annemann. Nearly 200 astonishing feats of mental magic revealed in step-by-step detail. Complete advice on staging, patter, etc. Illustrated. 320pp. 5⅜ × 8½. 24426-1 Pa. $5.95

CELEBRATED CASES OF JUDGE DEE (DEE GOONG AN), translated by Robert Van Gulik. Authentic 18th-century Chinese detective novel; Dee and associates solve three interlocked cases. Led to van Gulik's own stories with same characters. Extensive introduction. 9 illustrations. 237pp. 5⅜ × 8½. 23337-5 Pa. $4.50

CUT & FOLD EXTRATERRESTRIAL INVADERS THAT FLY, M. Grater. Stage your own lilliputian space battles.By following the step-by-step instructions and explanatory diagrams you can launch 22 full-color fliers into space. 36pp. 8¼ × 11. 24478-4 Pa. $2.95

CUT & ASSEMBLE VICTORIAN HOUSES, Edmund V. Gillon, Jr. Printed in full color on heavy cardboard stock, 4 authentic Victorian houses in H-O scale: Italian-style Villa, Octagon, Second Empire, Stick Style. 48pp. 9¼ × 12¼. 23849-0 Pa. $3.95

BEST SCIENCE FICTION STORIES OF H.G. WELLS, H.G. Wells. Full novel *The Invisible Man*, plus 17 short stories: "The Crystal Egg," "Aepyornis Island," "The Strange Orchid," etc. 303pp. 5⅜ × 8½. (Available in U.S. only) 21531-8 Pa. $3.95

TRADEMARK DESIGNS OF THE WORLD, Yusaku Kamekura. A lavish collection of nearly 700 trademarks, the work of Wright, Loewy, Klee, Binder, hundreds of others. 160pp. 8¾ × 8. (Available in U.S. only) 24191-2 Pa. $5.00

THE ARTIST'S AND CRAFTSMAN'S GUIDE TO REDUCING, ENLARGING AND TRANSFERRING DESIGNS, Rita Weiss. Discover, reduce, enlarge, transfer designs from any objects to any craft project. 12pp. plus 16 sheets special graph paper. 8¼ × 11. 24142-4 Pa. $3.25

TREASURY OF JAPANESE DESIGNS AND MOTIFS FOR ARTISTS AND CRAFTSMEN, edited by Carol Belanger Grafton. Indispensable collection of 360 traditional Japanese designs and motifs redrawn in clean, crisp black-and-white, copyright-free illustrations. 96pp. 8¼ × 11. 24435-0 Pa. $3.95

CHANCERY CURSIVE STROKE BY STROKE, Arthur Baker. Instructions and illustrations for each stroke of each letter (upper and lower case) and numerals. 54 full-page plates. 64pp. 8¼ × 11.   24278-1 Pa. $2.50

THE ENJOYMENT AND USE OF COLOR, Walter Sargent. Color relationships, values, intensities; complementary colors, illumination, similar topics. Color in nature and art. 7 color plates, 29 illustrations. 274pp. 5⅜ × 8½.   20944-X Pa. $4.50

SCULPTURE PRINCIPLES AND PRACTICE, Louis Slobodkin. Step-by-step approach to clay, plaster, metals, stone; classical and modern. 253 drawings, photos. 255pp. 8⅛ × 11.   22960-2 Pa. $7.00

VICTORIAN FASHION PAPER DOLLS FROM HARPER'S BAZAR, 1867-1898, Theodore Menten. Four female dolls with 28 elegant high fashion costumes, printed in full color. 32pp. 9¼ × 12¼.   23453-3 Pa. $3.50

FLOPSY, MOPSY AND COTTONTAIL: A Little Book of Paper Dolls in Full Color, Susan LaBelle. Three dolls and 21 costumes (7 for each doll) show Peter Rabbit's siblings dressed for holidays, gardening, hiking, etc. Charming borders, captions. 48pp. 4¼ × 5½.   24376-1 Pa. $2.00

NATIONAL LEAGUE BASEBALL CARD CLASSICS, Bert Randolph Sugar. 83 big-leaguers from 1909-69 on facsimile cards. Hubbell, Dean, Spahn, Brock plus advertising, info, no duplications. Perforated, detachable. 16pp. 8¼ × 11.
24308-7 Pa. $2.95

THE LOGICAL APPROACH TO CHESS, Dr. Max Euwe, et al. First-rate text of comprehensive strategy, tactics, theory for the amateur. No gambits to memorize, just a clear, logical approach. 224pp. 5⅜ × 8½.   24353-2 Pa. $4.50

MAGICK IN THEORY AND PRACTICE, Aleister Crowley. The summation of the thought and practice of the century's most famous necromancer, long hard to find. Crowley's best book. 436pp. 5⅜ × 8½. (Available in U.S. only)
23295-6 Pa. $6.50

THE HAUNTED HOTEL, Wilkie Collins. Collins' last great tale; doom and destiny in a Venetian palace. Praised by T.S. Eliot. 127pp. 5⅜ × 8½.
24333-8 Pa. $3.00

ART DECO DISPLAY ALPHABETS, Dan X. Solo. Wide variety of bold yet elegant lettering in handsome Art Deco styles. 100 complete fonts, with numerals, punctuation, more. 104pp. 8⅛ × 11.   24372-9 Pa. $4.00

CALLIGRAPHIC ALPHABETS, Arthur Baker. Nearly 150 complete alphabets by outstanding contemporary. Stimulating ideas; useful source for unique effects. 154 plates. 157pp. 8⅜ × 11¼.   21045-6 Pa. $4.95

ARTHUR BAKER'S HISTORIC CALLIGRAPHIC ALPHABETS, Arthur Baker. From monumental capitals of first-century Rome to humanistic cursive of 16th century, 33 alphabets in fresh interpretations. 88 plates. 96pp. 9 × 12.
24054-1 Pa. $3.95

LETTIE LANE PAPER DOLLS, Sheila Young. Genteel turn-of-the-century family very popular then and now. 24 paper dolls. 16 plates in full color. 32pp. 9¼ × 12¼.   24089-4 Pa. $3.50

KEYBOARD WORKS FOR SOLO INSTRUMENTS, G.F. Handel. 35 neglected works from Handel's vast oeuvre, originally jotted down as improvisations. Includes Eight Great Suites, others. New sequence. 174pp. 9⅜ × 12¼.
24338-9 Pa. $7.50

AMERICAN LEAGUE BASEBALL CARD CLASSICS, Bert Randolph Sugar. 82 stars from 1900s to 60s on facsimile cards. Ruth, Cobb, Mantle, Williams, plus advertising, info, no duplications. Perforated, detachable. 16pp. 8¼ × 11.
24286-2 Pa. $2.95

A TREASURY OF CHARTED DESIGNS FOR NEEDLEWORKERS, Georgia Gorham and Jeanne Warth. 141 charted designs: owl, cat with yarn, tulips, piano, spinning wheel, covered bridge, Victorian house and many others. 48pp. 8¼ × 11.
23558-0 Pa. $1.95

DANISH FLORAL CHARTED DESIGNS, Gerda Bengtsson. Exquisite collection of over 40 different florals: anemone, Iceland poppy, wild fruit, pansies, many others. 45 illustrations. 48pp. 8¼ × 11.
23957-8 Pa. $1.75

OLD PHILADELPHIA IN EARLY PHOTOGRAPHS 1839-1914, Robert F. Looney. 215 photographs: panoramas, street scenes, landmarks, President-elect Lincoln's visit, 1876 Centennial Exposition, much more. 230pp. 8⅞ × 11¾.
23345-6 Pa. $9.95

PRELUDE TO MATHEMATICS, W.W. Sawyer. Noted mathematician's lively, stimulating account of non-Euclidean geometry, matrices, determinants, group theory, other topics. Emphasis on novel, striking aspects. 224pp. 5⅜ × 8½.
24401-6 Pa. $4.50

ADVENTURES WITH A MICROSCOPE, Richard Headstrom. 59 adventures with clothing fibers, protozoa, ferns and lichens, roots and leaves, much more. 142 illustrations. 232pp. 5⅜ × 8½.
23471-1 Pa. $3.50

IDENTIFYING ANIMAL TRACKS: MAMMALS, BIRDS, AND OTHER ANIMALS OF THE EASTERN UNITED STATES, Richard Headstrom. For hunters, naturalists, scouts, nature-lovers. Diagrams of tracks, tips on identification. 128pp. 5⅜ × 8.
24442-3 Pa. $3.50

VICTORIAN FASHIONS AND COSTUMES FROM HARPER'S BAZAR, 1867-1898, edited by Stella Blum. Day costumes, evening wear, sports clothes, shoes, hats, other accessories in over 1,000 detailed engravings. 320pp. 9⅜ × 12¼.
22990-4 Pa. $9.95

EVERYDAY FASHIONS OF THE TWENTIES AS PICTURED IN SEARS AND OTHER CATALOGS, edited by Stella Blum. Actual dress of the Roaring Twenties, with text by Stella Blum. Over 750 illustrations, captions. 156pp. 9 × 12.
24134-3 Pa. $7.95

HALL OF FAME BASEBALL CARDS, edited by Bert Randolph Sugar. Cy Young, Ted Williams, Lou Gehrig, and many other Hall of Fame greats on 92 full-color, detachable reprints of early baseball cards. No duplication of cards with *Classic Baseball Cards*. 16pp. 8¼ × 11. 23624-2 Pa. $2.95

THE ART OF HAND LETTERING, Helm Wotzkow. Course in hand lettering, Roman, Gothic, Italic, Block, Script. Tools, proportions, optical aspects, individual variation. Very quality conscious. Hundreds of specimens. 320pp. 5⅜ × 8½.
21797-3 Pa. $4.95

HOW THE OTHER HALF LIVES, Jacob A. Riis. Journalistic record of filth, degradation, upward drive in New York immigrant slums, shops, around 1900. New edition includes 100 original Riis photos, monuments of early photography. 233pp. 10 × 7⅞. 22012-5 Pa. $7.95

CHINA AND ITS PEOPLE IN EARLY PHOTOGRAPHS, John Thomson. In 200 black-and-white photographs of exceptional quality photographic pioneer Thomson captures the mountains, dwellings, monuments and people of 19th-century China. 272pp. 9⅜ × 12¼. 24393-1 Pa. $12.95

GODEY COSTUME PLATES IN COLOR FOR DECOUPAGE AND FRAMING, edited by Eleanor Hasbrouk Rawlings. 24 full-color engravings depicting 19th-century Parisian haute couture. Printed on one side only. 56pp. 8¼ × 11. 23879-2 Pa. $3.95

ART NOUVEAU STAINED GLASS PATTERN BOOK, Ed Sibbett, Jr. 104 projects using well-known themes of Art Nouveau: swirling forms, florals, peacocks, and sensuous women. 60pp. 8¼ × 11. 23577-7 Pa. $3.00

QUICK AND EASY PATCHWORK ON THE SEWING MACHINE: Susan Aylsworth Murwin and Suzzy Payne. Instructions, diagrams show exactly how to machine sew 12 quilts. 48pp. of templates. 50 figures. 80pp. 8¼ × 11. 23770-2 Pa. $3.50

THE STANDARD BOOK OF QUILT MAKING AND COLLECTING, Marguerite Ickis. Full information, full-sized patterns for making 46 traditional quilts, also 150 other patterns. 483 illustrations. 273pp. 6⅞ × 9⅝. 20582-7 Pa. $5.95

LETTERING AND ALPHABETS, J. Albert Cavanagh. 85 complete alphabets lettered in various styles; instructions for spacing, roughs, brushwork. 121pp. 8¾ × 8. 20053-1 Pa. $3.75

LETTER FORMS: 110 COMPLETE ALPHABETS, Frederick Lambert. 110 sets of capital letters; 16 lower case alphabets; 70 sets of numbers and other symbols. 110pp. 8⅛ × 11. 22872-X Pa. $4.50

ORCHIDS AS HOUSE PLANTS, Rebecca Tyson Northen. Grow cattleyas and many other kinds of orchids—in a window, in a case, or under artificial light. 63 illustrations. 148pp. 5⅜ × 8½. 23261-1 Pa. $2.95

THE MUSHROOM HANDBOOK, Louis C.C. Krieger. Still the best popular handbook. Full descriptions of 259 species, extremely thorough text, poisons, folklore, etc. 32 color plates; 126 other illustrations. 560pp. 5⅜ × 8½. 21861-9 Pa. $8.50

THE DORÉ BIBLE ILLUSTRATIONS, Gustave Doré. All wonderful, detailed plates: Adam and Eve, Flood, Babylon, life of Jesus, etc. Brief King James text with each plate. 241 plates. 241pp. 9 × 12. 23004-X Pa. $6.95

THE BOOK OF KELLS: Selected Plates in Full Color, edited by Blanche Cirker. 32 full-page plates from greatest manuscript-icon of early Middle Ages. Fantastic, mysterious. Publisher's Note. Captions. 32pp. 9¾ × 12¼. 24345-1 Pa. $4.50

THE PERFECT WAGNERITE, George Bernard Shaw. Brilliant criticism of the Ring Cycle, with provocative interpretation of politics, economic theories behind the Ring. 136pp. 5⅜ × 8½. (Available in U.S. only) 21707-8 Pa. $3.00

CATALOG OF DOVER BOOKS

THE RIME OF THE ANCIENT MARINER, Gustave Doré, S.T. Coleridge. Doré's finest work, 34 plates capture moods, subtleties of poem. Full text. 77pp. 9¼ × 12. 22305-1 Pa. $4.95

SONGS OF INNOCENCE, William Blake. The first and most popular of Blake's famous "Illuminated Books," in a facsimile edition reproducing all 31 brightly colored plates. Additional printed text of each poem. 64pp. 5¼ × 7. 22764-2 Pa. $3.00

AN INTRODUCTION TO INFORMATION THEORY, J.R. Pierce. Second (1980) edition of most impressive non-technical account available. Encoding, entropy, noisy channel, related areas, etc. 320pp. 5⅜ × 8½. 24061-4 Pa. $4.95

THE DIVINE PROPORTION: A STUDY IN MATHEMATICAL BEAUTY, H.E. Huntley. "Divine proportion" or "golden ratio" in poetry, Pascal's triangle, philosophy, psychology, music, mathematical figures, etc. Excellent bridge between science and art. 58 figures. 185pp. 5⅜ × 8½. 22254-3 Pa. $3.95

THE DOVER NEW YORK WALKING GUIDE: From the Battery to Wall Street, Mary J. Shapiro. Superb inexpensive guide to historic buildings and locales in lower Manhattan: Trinity Church, Bowling Green, more. Complete Text; maps. 36 illustrations. 48pp. 3⅞ × 9¼. 24225-0 Pa. $1.75

NEW YORK THEN AND NOW, Edward B. Watson, Edmund V. Gillon, Jr. 83 important Manhattan sites: on facing pages early photographs (1875-1925) and 1976 photos by Gillon. 172 illustrations. 171pp. 9¼ × 10. 23361-8 Pa. $7.95

HISTORIC COSTUME IN PICTURES, Braun & Schneider. Over 1450 costumed figures from dawn of civilization to end of 19th century. English captions. 125 plates. 256pp. 8⅜ × 11¼. 23150-X Pa. $7.50

VICTORIAN AND EDWARDIAN FASHION; A Photographic Survey, Alison Gernsheim. First fashion history completely illustrated by contemporary photographs. Full text plus 235 photos, 1840-1914, in which many celebrities appear. 240pp. 6½ × 9¼. 24205-6 Pa. $6.00

CHARTED CHRISTMAS DESIGNS FOR COUNTED CROSS-STITCH AND OTHER NEEDLECRAFTS, Lindberg Press. Charted designs for 45 beautiful needlecraft projects with many yuletide and wintertime motifs. 48pp. 8¼ × 11. 24356-7 Pa. $1.95

101 FOLK DESIGNS FOR COUNTED CROSS-STITCH AND OTHER NEEDLE-CRAFTS, Carter Houck. 101 authentic charted folk designs in a wide array of lovely representations with many suggestions for effective use. 48pp. 8¼ × 11. 24369-9 Pa. $1.95

FIVE ACRES AND INDEPENDENCE, Maurice G. Kains. Great back-to-the-land classic explains basics of self-sufficient farming. The one book to get. 95 illustrations. 397pp. 5⅜ × 8½. 20974-1 Pa. $4.95

A MODERN HERBAL, Margaret Grieve. Much the fullest, most exact, most useful compilation of herbal material. Gigantic alphabetical encyclopedia, from aconite to zedoary, gives botanical information, medical properties, folklore, economic uses, and much else. Indispensable to serious reader. 161 illustrations. 888pp. 6½ × 9¼. (Available in U.S. only) 22798-7, 22799-5 Pa., Two-vol. set $16.45

DECORATIVE NAPKIN FOLDING FOR BEGINNERS, Lillian Oppenheimer and Natalie Epstein. 22 different napkin folds in the shape of a heart, clown's hat, love knot, etc. 63 drawings. 48pp. 8¼ × 11.   23797-4 Pa. $1.95

DECORATIVE LABELS FOR HOME CANNING, PRESERVING, AND OTHER HOUSEHOLD AND GIFT USES, Theodore Menten. 128 gummed, perforated labels, beautifully printed in 2 colors. 12 versions. Adhere to metal, glass, wood, ceramics. 24pp. 8¼ × 11.   23219-0 Pa. $2.95

EARLY AMERICAN STENCILS ON WALLS AND FURNITURE, Janet Waring. Thorough coverage of 19th-century folk art: techniques, artifacts, surviving specimens. 166 illustrations, 7 in color. 147pp. of text. 7⅞ × 10¾. 21906-2 Pa. $8.95

AMERICAN ANTIQUE WEATHERVANES, A.B. & W.T. Westervelt. Extensively illustrated 1883 catalog exhibiting over 550 copper weathervanes and finials. Excellent primary source by one of the principal manufacturers. 104pp. 6⅛ × 9¼.   24396-6 Pa. $3.95

ART STUDENTS' ANATOMY, Edmond J. Farris. Long favorite in art schools. Basic elements, common positions, actions. Full text, 158 illustrations. 159pp. 5⅜ × 8½.   20744-7 Pa. $3.50

BRIDGMAN'S LIFE DRAWING, George B. Bridgman. More than 500 drawings and text teach you to abstract the body into its major masses. Also specific areas of anatomy. 192pp. 6½ × 9¼. (EA)   22710-3 Pa. $4.50

COMPLETE PRELUDES AND ETUDES FOR SOLO PIANO, Frederic Chopin. All 26 Preludes, all 27 Etudes by greatest composer of piano music. Authoritative Paderewski edition. 224pp. 9 × 12. (Available in U.S. only)   24052-5 Pa. $6.95

PIANO MUSIC 1888-1905, Claude Debussy. Deux Arabesques, Suite Bergamesque, Masques, 1st series of Images, etc. 9 others, in corrected editions. 175pp. 9⅜ × 12¼.   (ECE) 22771-5 Pa. $5.95

TEDDY BEAR IRON-ON TRANSFER PATTERNS, Ted Menten. 80 iron-on transfer patterns of male and female Teddys in a wide variety of activities, poses, sizes. 48pp. 8¼ × 11.   24596-9 Pa. $2.00

A PICTURE HISTORY OF THE BROOKLYN BRIDGE, M.J. Shapiro. Profusely illustrated account of greatest engineering achievement of 19th century. 167 rare photos & engravings recall construction, human drama. Extensive, detailed text. 122pp. 8¼ × 11.   24403-2 Pa. $7.95

NEW YORK IN THE THIRTIES, Berenice Abbott. Noted photographer's fascinating study shows new buildings that have become famous and old sights that have disappeared forever. 97 photographs. 97pp. 11⅜ × 10.   22967-X Pa. $6.50

MATHEMATICAL TABLES AND FORMULAS, Robert D. Carmichael and Edwin R. Smith. Logarithms, sines, tangents, trig functions, powers, roots, reciprocals, exponential and hyperbolic functions, formulas and theorems. 269pp. 5⅜ × 8½.   60111-0 Pa. $3.75

HANDBOOK OF MATHEMATICAL FUNCTIONS WITH FORMULAS, GRAPHS, AND MATHEMATICAL TABLES, edited by Milton Abramowitz and Irene A. Stegun. Vast compendium: 29 sets of tables, some to as high as 20 places. 1,046pp. 8 × 10½.   61272-4 Pa. $19.95

REASON IN ART, George Santayana. Renowned philosopher's provocative, seminal treatment of basis of art in instinct and experience. Volume Four of *The Life of Reason*. 230pp. 5⅜ × 8. 24358-3 Pa. $4.50

LANGUAGE, TRUTH AND LOGIC, Alfred J. Ayer. Famous, clear introduction to Vienna, Cambridge schools of Logical Positivism. Role of philosophy, elimination of metaphysics, nature of analysis, etc. 160pp. 5⅜ × 8½. (USCO) 20010-8 Pa. $2.75

BASIC ELECTRONICS, U.S. Bureau of Naval Personnel. Electron tubes, circuits, antennas, AM, FM, and CW transmission and receiving, etc. 560 illustrations. 567pp. 6½ × 9¼. 21076-6 Pa. $8.95

THE ART DECO STYLE, edited by Theodore Menten. Furniture, jewelry, metalwork, ceramics, fabrics, lighting fixtures, interior decors, exteriors, graphics from pure French sources. Over 400 photographs. 183pp. 8⅜ × 11¼. 22824-X Pa. $6.95

THE FOUR BOOKS OF ARCHITECTURE, Andrea Palladio. 16th-century classic covers classical architectural remains, Renaissance revivals, classical orders, etc. 1738 Ware English edition. 216 plates. 110pp. of text. 9½ × 12¾. 21308-0 Pa. $10.00

THE WIT AND HUMOR OF OSCAR WILDE, edited by Alvin Redman. More than 1000 ripostes, paradoxes, wisecracks: Work is the curse of the drinking classes, I can resist everything except temptations, etc. 258pp. 5⅜ × 8½. (USCO) 20602-5 Pa. $3.50

THE DEVIL'S DICTIONARY, Ambrose Bierce. Barbed, bitter, brilliant witticisms in the form of a dictionary. Best, most ferocious satire America has produced. 145pp. 5⅜ × 8½. 20487-1 Pa. $2.50

ERTÉ'S FASHION DESIGNS, Erté. 210 black-and-white inventions from *Harper's Bazar*, 1918-32, plus 8pp. full-color covers. Captions. 88pp. 9 × 12. 24203-X Pa. $6.50

ERTÉ GRAPHICS, Erté. Collection of striking color graphics: *Seasons, Alphabet, Numerals, Aces* and *Precious Stones*. 50 plates, including 4 on covers. 48pp. 9⅜ × 12¼. 23580-7 Pa. $6.95

PAPER FOLDING FOR BEGINNERS, William D. Murray and Francis J. Rigney. Clearest book for making origami sail boats, roosters, frogs that move legs, etc. 40 projects. More than 275 illustrations. 94pp. 5⅜ × 8½. 20713-7 Pa. $1.95

ORIGAMI FOR THE ENTHUSIAST, John Montroll. Fish, ostrich, peacock, squirrel, rhinoceros, Pegasus, 19 other intricate subjects. Instructions. Diagrams. 128pp. 9 × 12. 23799-0 Pa. $4.95

CROCHETING NOVELTY POT HOLDERS, edited by Linda Macho. 64 useful, whimsical pot holders feature kitchen themes, animals, flowers, other novelties. Surprisingly easy to crochet. Complete instructions. 48pp. 8¼ × 11. 24296-X Pa. $1.95

CROCHETING DOILIES, edited by Rita Weiss. Irish Crochet, Jewel, Star Wheel, Vanity Fair and more. Also luncheon and console sets, runners and centerpieces. 51 illustrations. 48pp. 8¼ × 11. 23424-X Pa. $2.00

YUCATAN BEFORE AND AFTER THE CONQUEST, Diego de Landa. Only significant account of Yucatan written in the early post-Conquest era. Translated by William Gates. Over 120 illustrations. 162pp. 5⅜ × 8½. 23622-6 Pa. $3.50

ORNATE PICTORIAL CALLIGRAPHY, E.A. Lupfer. Complete instructions, over 150 examples help you create magnificent "flourishes" from which beautiful animals and objects gracefully emerge. 8⅛ × 11. 21957-7 Pa. $2.95

DOLLY DINGLE PAPER DOLLS, Grace Drayton. Cute chubby children by same artist who did Campbell Kids. Rare plates from 1910s. 30 paper dolls and over 100 outfits reproduced in full color. 32pp. 9¼ × 12¼. 23711-7 Pa. $2.95

CURIOUS GEORGE PAPER DOLLS IN FULL COLOR, H. A. Rey, Kathy Allert. Naughty little monkey-hero of children's books in two doll figures, plus 48 full-color costumes: pirate, Indian chief, fireman, more. 32pp. 9¼ × 12¼. 24386-9 Pa. $3.50

GERMAN: HOW TO SPEAK AND WRITE IT, Joseph Rosenberg. Like *French, How to Speak and Write It.* Very rich modern course, with a wealth of pictorial material. 330 illustrations. 384pp. 5⅜ × 8½. (USUKO) 20271-2 Pa. $4.75

CATS AND KITTENS: 24 Ready-to-Mail Color Photo Postcards, D. Holby. Handsome collection; feline in a variety of adorable poses. Identifications. 12pp. on postcard stock. 8¼ × 11. 24469-5 Pa. $2.95

MARILYN MONROE PAPER DOLLS, Tom Tierney. 31 full-color designs on heavy stock, from *The Asphalt Jungle, Gentlemen Prefer Blondes,* 22 others. 1 doll. 16 plates. 32pp. 9⅜ × 12¼. 23769-9 Pa. $3.50

FUNDAMENTALS OF LAYOUT, F.H. Wills. All phases of layout design discussed and illustrated in 121 illustrations. Indispensable as student's text or handbook for professional. 124pp. 8⅛.× 11. 21279-3 Pa. $4.50

FANTASTIC SUPER STICKERS, Ed Sibbett, Jr. 75 colorful pressure-sensitive stickers. Peel off and place for a touch of pizzazz: clowns, penguins, teddy bears, etc. Full color. 16pp. 8¼ × 11. 24471-7 Pa. $2.95

LABELS FOR ALL OCCASIONS, Ed Sibbett, Jr. 6 labels each of 16 different designs—baroque, art nouveau, art deco, Pennsylvania Dutch, etc.—in full color. 24pp. 8¼ × 11. 23688-9 Pa. $2.95

HOW TO CALCULATE QUICKLY: RAPID METHODS IN BASIC MATHEMATICS, Henry Sticker. Addition, subtraction, multiplication, division, checks, etc. More than 8000 problems, solutions. 185pp. 5 × 7¼. 20295-X Pa. $2.95

THE CAT COLORING BOOK, Karen Baldauski. Handsome, realistic renderings of 40 splendid felines, from American shorthair to exotic types. 44 plates. Captions. 48pp. 8¼ × 11. 24011-8 Pa. $2.25

THE TALE OF PETER RABBIT, Beatrix Potter. The inimitable Peter's terrifying adventure in Mr. McGregor's garden, with all 27 wonderful, full-color Potter illustrations. 55pp. 4¼ × 5½. (Available in U.S. only) 22827-4 Pa. $1.50

BASIC ELECTRICITY, U.S. Bureau of Naval Personnel. Batteries, circuits, conductors, AC and DC, inductance and capacitance, generators, motors, transformers, amplifiers, etc. 349 illustrations. 448pp. 6½ × 9¼. 20973-3 Pa. $7.95

SOURCE BOOK OF MEDICAL HISTORY, edited by Logan Clendening, M.D. Original accounts ranging from Ancient Egypt and Greece to discovery of X-rays: Galen, Pasteur, Lavoisier, Harvey, Parkinson, others. 685pp. 5⅜ × 8½.
20621-1 Pa. $10.95

THE ROSE AND THE KEY, J.S. Lefanu. Superb mystery novel from Irish master. Dark doings among an ancient and aristocratic English family. Well-drawn characters; capital suspense. Introduction by N. Donaldson. 448pp. 5⅜ × 8½.
24377-X Pa. $6.95

SOUTH WIND, Norman Douglas. Witty, elegant novel of ideas set on languorous Mediterranean island of Nepenthe. Elegant prose, glittering epigrams, mordant satire. 1917 masterpiece. 416pp. 5⅜ × 8½. (Available in U.S. only)
24361-3 Pa. $5.95

RUSSELL'S CIVIL WAR PHOTOGRAPHS, Capt. A.J. Russell. 116 rare Civil War Photos: Bull Run, Virginia campaigns, bridges, railroads, Richmond, Lincoln's funeral car. Many never seen before. Captions. 128pp. 9⅜ × 12¼.
24283-8 Pa. $6.95

PHOTOGRAPHS BY MAN RAY: 105 Works, 1920-1934. Nudes, still lifes, landscapes, women's faces, celebrity portraits (Dali, Matisse, Picasso, others), rayographs. Reprinted from rare gravure edition. 128pp. 9⅜ × 12¼. (Available in U.S. only)
23842-3 Pa. $6.95

STAR NAMES: THEIR LORE AND MEANING, Richard H. Allen. Star names, the zodiac, constellations: folklore and literature associated with heavens. The basic book of its field, fascinating reading. 563pp. 5⅜ × 8½.
21079-0 Pa. $7.95

BURNHAM'S CELESTIAL HANDBOOK, Robert Burnham, Jr. Thorough guide to the stars beyond our solar system. Exhaustive treatment. Alphabetical by constellation: Andromeda to Cetus in Vol. 1; Chamaeleon to Orion in Vol. 2; and Pavo to Vulpecula in Vol. 3. Hundreds of illustrations. Index in Vol. 3. 2000pp. 6⅛ × 9¼.
23567-X, 23568-8, 23673-0 Pa. Three-vol. set $32.85

THE ART NOUVEAU STYLE BOOK OF ALPHONSE MUCHA, Alphonse Mucha. All 72 plates from *Documents Decoratifs* in original color. Stunning, essential work of Art Nouveau. 80pp. 9⅜ × 12¼.
24044-4 Pa. $7.95

DESIGNS BY ERTE; FASHION DRAWINGS AND ILLUSTRATIONS FROM "HARPER'S BAZAR," Erte. 310 fabulous line drawings and 14 *Harper's Bazar* covers, 8 in full color. Erte's exotic temptresses with tassels, fur muffs, long trains, coifs, more. 129pp. 9⅜ × 12¼.
23397-9 Pa. $6.95

HISTORY OF STRENGTH OF MATERIALS, Stephen P. Timoshenko. Excellent historical survey of the strength of materials with many references to the theories of elasticity and structure. 245 figures. 452pp. 5⅜ × 8½. 61187-6 Pa. $8.95

Prices subject to change without notice.
Available at your book dealer or write for free catalog to Dept. GI, Dover Publications, Inc., 31 East 2nd St. Mineola, N.Y. 11501. Dover publishes more than 175 books each year on science, elementary and advanced mathematics, biology, music, art, literary history, social sciences and other areas.